The Icelandic Unitarian Connection

Beginnings of Icelandic Unitarianism in North America, 1885-1900

by
V. Emil Gudmundson, B.D.,D.D.

**Completed posthumously by
Barbara J.R. Gudmundson, Ph.D.,
Editor in Chief; and
G. Eric Bjornson, B.A., B.Ed.,Editor**

**With a Foreword by
Conrad Wright
Professor of American Church History,
The Divinity School, Harvard University**

wheatfield press

winnipeg, manitoba

ISBN 0-920374-08-5

Publisher: Wheatfield Press, Winnipeg, MB
Book Design and Layout: Eric Jonasson
Cover Artwork: Charles O.J. Jonasson
Typesetting/Printing: Industrial Art and Printing, Winnipeg, MB

General book text was set using
10pt. Times Roman typeface on a 12pt. leading.
Chapter heading decorations are from the designs
of an unknown 13th century Icelandic manuscript illustrator.

Distributed in Canada by
Wheatfield Press, Box 205, St. James P.O.,
Winnipeg, MB, R3J 3R4

Distributed in the U.S.A. by
Unitarian Universalist Assn., 25 Beacon St., Boston, MA 02108;
and (for western orders) Barbara R. Gudmundson,
Box 17102, Minneapolis, MN 55417.

Made in Canada

Canadian Cataloguing in Publication Data

Gudmundson, V. Emil (Valtýr Emil), 1924-1982.

The Icelandic Unitarian Connection

(Minns lectures, 1981)

"Magnús Eiríksson bibliography": p.
Includes index.
ISBN 0-920374-08-5

1. Unitarian Universalist Association — History. 2. Icelandic Canadians — History. 3. Icelandic Americans — History. I. Title. II. Series.

BX9831.G83 1984   288'.32   C84-091526-8

48, 220

Dedication

I want to make a dedication of these lectures to five women,

all major influences in my life,

who have not only been supportive of me in my independence of mind

and thought, and my endeavors,

but loving and honest—and even gadflies—in their relationships with me,

each a different kind of prod and support.

Mekkín Jónsdóttir Guðmundsson

my grandmother, who, in my family account, is the first Unitarian;

Rannveig Dorothea Thorsteinsson Gudmundson

my mother, who was always the teacher, and never let us get by

with anything sloppily done when it came to learning;

Barbara Jane Rohrke Gudmundson

my wife, who is the scientist and the scholar in the family; and

Holly Mekkín and Martha Rannveig Gudmundson

my daughters, the questioners and inquisitors in the family.

— V. Emil Gudmundson, 1981

Acknowledgements

It is difficult — or impossible — to list all those who had helped Emil in his researching and writing of this book; it is much simpler to draw up a list of those who helped me complete it. But both of us were very fortunate to have had the support of so many capable and helpful friends and, because I am so grateful to them, I am willing to take the risk inherent in the specifying of names: finding later that deserving names have been omitted. I hope that those whose names are not on this list and should be will let me know of their involvement. Perhaps I will be able to find a way to give them the credit they deserve.

The Veatch Program Board of Governors, The Minns Lecture Committee, The Unitarian Universalist Association, The Unitarian Universalist Historical Society Collegium, and The Can-Am Prairie Interdistrict Committee.

Prof. Haraldur Bessason, Vilhjalmur Bjarnar, Eric and Margaret Bjornson, Valdimar Bjornson, Helen Bullard, Dr. Paul Carnes, Hilary Cummings, Dr. John and Drusilla Cummins, Nina Draxten, Joan Fagerlie, Rev. Neil Gerdes, Dr. John Gilbert, Dr. Thomas Graham, Eyrún Gudmundsdóttir,Dr. Finnbogi Gudmundsson, Rannveig, Bjorn and Leslie Gudmundson, Laufey Gudmundson, Dr. Óskar Halldórsson, Judith Hamilton, Ólafur Hjartar, Aleph and Lincoln Johansson, Sigrid Johnson, Eric Jónasson, Stefán Jónasson, Kristine Kristoffersson, Dr. Spencer Lavan, Palmi Pálsson, Dr. Eugene Pickett, Dr. Philip M. Pétursson, Hermina Poatgieter, Doris Pullen, Rev. Alan Seaburg, Rev. Carl Seaburg, Edith Bjornson Sunley, Rúnolfur Thorarinsson, Jón Thorsteinsson, Rev. Richard Woodman, Dr. Conrad Wright, Trevor Holm, and Rev. Charlotte Cowtan-Holm.

Thank you all for the essential help you have given to this project.

B.R.G.

Table of Contents

Appendixes

Photograph/Map Section begins on page 82.

Foreword

Few Unitarian Universalists, unless they happened to live in Manitoba or Minnesota, have ever been aware of the existence of Icelandic Unitarian churches, and their story has scarcely been acknowledged in general accounts of the denomination. Fifty years ago, Dr. George F. Patterson prepared an article for the **Proceedings** of the Unitarian Historical Society, but that item stands almost alone. This neglect is perhaps explainable: Winnipeg is a long way from Boston; the Icelandic churches have been small, usually rural, and limited in number; and Americans are not exactly fluent in Icelandic.

But the story of the Icelandic churches is a special one, which serves as a useful counterpoint in the history of the denomination. Lutheran rather than Puritan Calvinist in derivation, Scandinavian rather than New England or English in origin, Icelandic Unitarianism is a salutary reminder that liberal religion is not the special preserve of one ethnic or language group, and that there is more than one pathway of discovery. Bjorn Petursson and Magnus Skaptason are not going to occupy as large a place in our memory as Channing or Emerson or Bellows; but room should be made for them along with those others whose names we at least remember, even though their chief contribution to the cause of liberal religion was regional or local rather than denomination-wide.

Emil Gudmundson was uniquely qualified to make this special story available to us. Himself of Icelandic stock, he possessed the necessary language facility. A parish minister and then district executive, he nevertheless possessed strong scholarly interests and temperament. Persuaded to undertake the task that no one else could do so well, he spent six weeks in Iceland in the winter of 1979-80, working in the Landbokasafn; he found time to use the collections in Chicago at the Meadville Theological School; and whenever his duties brought him to Boston, he tried to save a few hours for research in the records of the American Unitarian Association at the Andover-Harvard Library. Here Alan Seaburg and I were privileged to exchange notes with him, and to share his pleasure in the discoveries he was making.

The materials Emil gathered formed the basis for the Minns Lectures delivered in 1981. The work was far from complete at the time of his death in 1982. The lectures came down to 1900, and a continuation of the story would have followed; and besides, he had not had a chance to rework and polish the manuscript. No doubt he would have been distressed at the thought that his incomplete work would be published without the perfecting care he would have given it. What we have falls short of his own standards. But incomplete and unpolished as it is, the work tells a story that needs to be made part of our common memories. So for what he aspired to do for us we salute Emil Gudmundson; and for what he was able to accomplish, though less than his desire, we are grateful.

CONRAD WRIGHT
Professor of American History,
The Divinity School, Harvard University.

Cambridge, Massachusetts
July 27, 1984.

Editorial Commentary

The preparation of the 1981 Minns Lectures by the late Rev. Dr. V. Emil Gudmundson emanated from his research for **The Icelandic Unitarian Connection** . As it happened, the lectures were prepared and delivered before the manuscript for the book was ready for printing. Fortunately, all the lectures were recorded on tape at the time of delivery. The tape transcripts have been utilized in completing those parts of the book which were incomplete at the time of the author's untimely death. Barbara Gudmundson, wife of the author, supplied the tape transcripts. Assisted by Helen Bullard, she also did invaluable work in the preliminary editing of them and their integration subsequently into the appropriate chapters of the book. This has been accomplished with minimal redundancy, although there are some instances of repetition which could not easily be avoided in the context.

A few words about the structure of the book seem appropriate. It was decided to print some of Emil's introduction to the Minns Lectures in the front part of the book because it establishes the personal tone of the author's involvement. Then, again, in the book's appendices the reader will find material which supplements the text in unique and interesting ways. Appendix G is an autobiographic account of Emil's origin as a Unitarian. Appendix H, a paper delivered by Emil in 1979, pre-examines some of the material to be found in this book; although it contains some redundancies, it also clarifies some aspects of **The Icelandic Unitarian Connection.** Appendix I is included because it provides the reader with an insight into the spread of Unitarianism through numerous Icelandic settlements on the North American continent. During his preparation of this book, Emil once indicated to me that he hoped to write a sequel to it. This sequel would undoubtedly have dealt in detail with the material to be found in Stefan Jonasson's letter to Barbara Gudmundson. (Appendix I). All-in-all, it seems imperative to advise the reader to consider the reading of the appendices as an essential and worthwhile adjunct to the reading of the ten basic chapters.

Because of the predominantly Icelandic aspect of **The Icelandic Unitarian Connection**, it was deemed proper to use the Icelandic spelling for numerous proper nouns which appear in these pages. The Icelandic alphabet contains 10 letters in addition to the 26 letters of the English alphabet. Their description and their sounds are dealt with in Appendix K. Finally, the reader is advised that maps are provided so that he/she can orientate various place names with the content of the book.

G. Eric Bjornson

Introduction to
The 1981 Minns Lectures

delivered in the Unitarian-Universalist Church of Winnipeg
and the Unitarian Church of Arborg in 1981
by
V. Emil Gudmundson

The Minns Lectures are sponsored by a 1938 bequest of the late Susan Minns of Boston, Massachusetts in honor of her brother and of the first minister of the First Church in Boston, a congregation established in 1630. She specified in her will that a joint management committee be set up by the First Church and King's Chapel, both Unitarian churches in Boston. The committee was charged to assure that six lectures be given annually on religion or religious subjects by Unitarian ministers in good standing. At that time, the lectures were given only in Boston.

Ten years ago, a desire to make the lectureship more widely known and of greater value to liberal religion led the two churches to take steps to diversify its program, expand its scope, and encourage presentation of the lectures in other parts of North America. Provision was made also for funding of more than one series per year, more lectures than six in a series, and other features designed to assist the lecturers and the distribution of the lectures. The presentation of the 1981 Minns Lectures at the center of Icelandic Unitarianism was made possible by this recent change.

BJRG

Tonight is a very special time, and of course it would be when one is reaping the fruits of a long research. But it's all the more so to have the honor of delivering a noted lecture within Unitarian Universalism. It is also special because it is "coming home" — a home-coming in at least two ways: It is coming home to the locus of Icelandic Unitarianism right here in Winnipeg, and I would not be "coming home" had it not been for the generous support of the United Conferences of Icelandic Churches in North America to study for the ministry back in the 40's. And among those who were my faithful and staunch supporters, and who still is and to whom I owe a great deal, is Philip Pétursson. So, Phil, thank you.

I could name others, but will name only one other who was a supporter and advocate at that time whom very few may have known, Bergthor Emil (Beggi) Johnson, the father of Lilja Arnason whom you know, and grandfather of my colleague, Wayne Arnason. 2 We're so proud to have him in the ministry. It was taken for granted that, after study first in Iceland and then in Chicago, I would return to serve one of these churches up here. 3 But post-war circumstances altered those prospects, and I have not ever served a church in Canada; and, perhaps, in all those years I have preached but one Icelandic sermon. But that's okay because now the Icelanders wouldn't understand it. 4 My present position, as Interdistrict Representative, is a foot in the door. But I must admit here publicly that I've always harbored a little regret — and even a little guilt — that I have never served a church here. And so tonight I am **"home"**, to tell myself, if no one else, that it **does** matter what happened in the past. I come here to repay the old debt of being helped by so many friends and relatives and Unitarians in this area to pursue my path to the ministry. I have come back to record the Icelandic Unitarian heritage.

And there is also a second sense in which this is a homecoming in a very personal way: Nothing I have ever done — no, nothing, has brought me such a sense of my own personal identity as has been done by this research and by the preparation of these lectures. Once in a while you're asked, "If there were only one or two things you could say about yourself, what would you tell people about yourself?"

Well, I find that I always have the same answer : "I'm Icelandic, I'm a Unitarian Universalist minister, and I'm a political liberal, if not a radical." And so, in a sense, this research, this probing, has put it all together for me and it has been no mere head trip, but really has been a trip of the total being and the soul. The people in my studies have been very real to me whether their names were Pétursson or Skaptason or Southworth or Forbush. I've learned a lot about my roots; I've learned a lot about the Unitarians and the Icelanders here. I've discovered some things about my own **self.** In digging through some of this material, I've discovered my mother's lineage is replete with clergy. I knew of only one of them, a great-uncle in Alberta, but I discovered, for instance, in all this study that my mother's uncle was the first to be exempted from his preparatory schooling before he entererd the School of

Theology. I took an immediate liking to him because here I am, all these generations later, having graduated from theological school without ever having had an undergraduate degree. So somehow, you know, he is a soul-mate.

And I have shared the walks through the snow that Björn Pétursson took in Pembina County. He knocked on the doors and whenever he got two together in the kitchen, he would preach them a sermon, probably translated from Kristofer Janson. I know only too well the New Icelandic spring mud that Magnús Skaptason talked about as he had to get off his horse and walk from Hnausa to Gimli. I know about the perverse wind and rain on Lake Winnipeg, so I too took Franklin Southworth's eleven-hour trip from the time he embarked on the lake until he got to Gimli. I've ridden the trains with T.B. Forbush and sweltered in the July heat with him here in Winnipeg, and stayed in the then fabulous new Leland Hotel. 5 Yes, I've even transported myself to Iceland, that country that my grandparents left, and broadened my acquaintance with the last century, and lived with the religious liberals whether they were the intellectual types and cynics in Reykjavík or Matthías Jochumsson of Akureyri, or some of the heretics at Seyðisfjörður.

This has been more than a labor of love. 6 It has been my life, in some sense, for the last year, and maybe my job has even suffered. Who knows?

I cannot recall fully how it all began, but that matters little. I'm glad that it **did** begin.

Just a word before I get into some substantive things: I'd like to describe briefly my methodology, for I make no claim to be a trained or professional historian. My major reason for this undertaking is that I have discovered in my reading of many of the historical essays that exist, that there are omissions and discrepancies. For example there is some uncertainty about the date on which Björn Pétursson was actually born. In addition, most of the researches were in Icelandic that were not easily available and of little use to, for example, Philip Hewett, 7 when he wrote his **History of Unitarians in Canada.** It therefore became my objective to probe all the original material I could find: newspaper accounts, correspondence, sermons, lectures, etc. of the period 1885 to 1900. And little did I know that in six lectures I can hardly get everything in — I **cannot** get everything in from that 15-year period. I found goldmine after goldmine of material. Luck or fate or grace — whatever you want to call it — was mine. It was my good fortune that the American Unitarian Association in Boston kept all the correspondence from the period of the 1880's and 90's, in fact, from all the periods; and all the old material is in the library of the Harvard Divinity School. And **there** are letters from Björn Pétursson, from Magnús Skaptason, from some of the lay people of this church, [8] both when they liked the way things were going with the minister, and when they didn't like it, back in the 90's, and reports on a regular basis from Kristofer Janson about his Icelandic mission. And I might also mention that the University of Manitoba Icelandic Library has every periodical and newspaper that I would want, and those were of great, great assistance. It is also where the Stephan G. Stephansson collection and numerous other things that were valuable to me are located. And then things had a way of slipping out of this country back to the old country, and the National Archives of Iceland have been the depository of letters and records such as the original record books from this very congregation [9], and from the congregation of Magnús Skaptason at Hnausa. And I have discovered other materials in attics and bookshelves here and there and made many friends while probing through the dusty tomes and sheets of paper that they've had.

Everywhere I've been well received, and in more than half the lectures I will refer almost exclusively to the fruits of these discoveries. Although I am well aware that some of this same material has been worked up by others, I have not relied upon the secondary sources. You would find, however, that there are similarities in them.

And now, to conclude these introductory remarks, I want to offer some words of appreciation for a few people. I only regret that Edith Björnsson Sunley of Manhasset, New York is not present. She is the granddaughter of Björn Pétursson, the daughter of the late Dr. Ólafur Björnsson of Winnipeg. Her enthusiasm has been unmatched and I have boxes of material that Edith has sent me. And her prodding and her telephone calls and her great assistance in helping me get a grant have been unmatched. And perhaps, second to her, I would mention her 98-year old cousin Aleph Johansson of Seattle, Washington who is very enthusiastic and very alert and has kept up a great interest and has given me a lot of material on Pétursson's wife Jennie. And then, briefly I **must** mention the librarians. What would I do without these librarians? I would not have found any of this material!

And now for the substance:

1. Rev. Philip M. Petursson D.D., Minister Emeritus of the Winnipeg Unitarian-Universalist Church.

2. Rev. Wayne Arnason, formerly of Winnipeg, currently employed with the U.U.A.

3. Unitarian Churches in Icelandic communities in North America.

4. Many second and third generation "Icelanders" in North America do not speak Icelandic.

5. An inner-city hotel in Winnipeg frequented by Icelanders.

6. Preparing the 1981 Minns Lectures and the manuscript for this book.

7. Rev. Philip Hewett, Unitarian clergyman in Western Canada.

8. The Winnipeg Unitarian Universalist Church where five of the six Minns Lectures were delivered.

9. See note 8 above.

GEB

Author's Preface

American Unitarianism of the latter half of the nineteenth century was a religion largely rooted in New England and New Englanders, although there were significant exceptions such as Philadelphia and Charleston, S.C. Even as Unitarianism found its way westward to Ohio, Illinois, Missouri, and California, it was primarily New Englanders who established new Unitarian churches. Frequently they counted among their numbers intellectual, cultural, philanthropic, and civic leaders.

The post-Civil War period (1865 - 1900) in the United States was a rich one in intellectual and religious thought. It was at once a time that can best be described as contentious and divisive, but also challenging and productive of growth. The people who moved west tended often to question the old expressions and old formulas, producing a ferment that gave birth to many movements and organizations such as the Free Religious Association. One organization that benefitted from this ferment was the Western Unitarian Conference, organized in 1852, which included all churches between the Alleghanies and the Rockies. By the last quarter of the century, the Western Conference was outspoken in their resistance to being identified with the old Christian principles of Boston Unitarianism. In the following excerpt, historian Conrad Wright notes the nature of the ferment — that, although it was cultural in general, it had specific relationships to the Unitarianism of the day:

> The second half of the nineteenth century was marked by an accelerated tendency in Western thought to interpret phenomena in historical or developmental terms, and no religious body was more sensitive to this tendency than the Unitarians. They were receptive to it in many different forms and manifestations; evolutionary thought, Spencerian or Darwinian; German Idealism, particularly with a Hegelian flavoring; Biblical

criticism, which gave a developmental account of the shaping of the Bible, and a persuasive reconstruction of the history of the religion of Israel; a version of the eighteenth-century idea of progress, which, to be sure, could be vulgarized into praise of material growth or support of Manifest Destiny; romantic notions of human nature, in which the capacity for spiritual growth was considered to be innate in every individual, a concept likewise subject to vulgarization at Unitarian hands, in the novels of the Reverend Horatio Alger Jr.

These concepts, often in their better, sometimes in their worse forms were assimilated without difficulty, across the whole range of Unitarian groups and factions: there is no significant difference, for example, between the reception of Darwinian evolution by Radicals and by conservatives. This developmental way of looking at religious ideas and institutions undercut equally the Absolute Religion of Theodore Parker and the static rationalism of Andrew Norton. The conflict between Christian Theist and Free Religionist was not eliminated, but its sharpness was moderated by an infusion of historical relativism. By emphasizing the relationship to Christianity as one of cherished historical continuity, rather than adherence to particular doctrinal formulations, the denomination avoided serious internal disruption as it moved into an age of secularism in which Christian motifs were increasingly bleached out of American Protestantism generally. More important for Unitarians at the close of the century than their long-standing differences was the common acceptance of an all-pervasive evolutionary optimism, so that conservative and radical alike could join in accepting at least the fifth of James Freeman Clarke's Five Points of Unitarian Belief: "The progress of mankind onward and upward forever." [1]

One does not, however, think of a Midwest Unitarian Church of this time to be a symbol of the melting pot, that is, of assimilating immigrants of a liberal persuasion into Unitarianism. One need only note that German immigrants often had religious-liberal ideas with which the Unitarians had little close contact. One of the earlier exceptions was the Norwegian Mission of Kristofer Janson begun in Minneapolis and Brown County, MN in 1880-81. Considering the tens of thousands of Norwegians who had emigrated, Janson's Mission was hardly a large movement numerically within this ethnic group. It was for Unitarianism at least a token as well as a beginning of trying to reach out to non-English speaking immigrants,culminating some twenty years later in a Department of New Americans in the American Unitarian Association (A.U.A.) in Boston.

In the late 1880's the beginnings of another ethnic Unitarian Mission and movement appeared, and became the most significant Unitarian outpost among ethnic liberals on this continent, namely the Icelandic settlers in Canada and the United States. This author has a very personal interest in this group, for he is a product of this movement.*

As a young man growing up on the Manitoba prairies during the Depression I little realized the significance of this movement, for I took the Unitarian presence for granted. After all, there were eight congregations with church buildings in Manitoba and Saskatchewan, and they formed the "United Conference of Icelandic Churches in North America." Our little congregation at Lundar had a minister, Guðmundur Árnason, a graduate of the Meadville Theological School and a Crufts Fellow. Several other ministers who served the Conference churches, in addition served as many as ten preaching stations. An old family friend and minister, the Reverend Albert E. Kristjánsson, reminisced in a letter in 1960, "I remember vividly our old battleground: Lundar, Mary Hill, Oak Point, Clarkleigh, Otto, Markland, Hove, Lillesve, Dog Creek, The Narrows, Siglunes, Reykjavik, Gargan, Langruth, etc."2

It is the author's purpose to explore the beginnings of this movement as thoroughly as is possible almost a century later,

*See Appendix G

for what is known and recorded is often based upon memories and not original sources, and contains numerous gaps as well as a few discrepancies.

1. Conrad Wright, "Salute the Arriving Moment" in **A Stream of Light — A Sesquicentennial History of American Unitarianism,** Conrad Wright, editor. Boston: Unitarian Universalist Association, 1975 pp. 93-94.

2. A personal letter to the author from the Rev. Albert E. Kristjánsson (1877-1974), dated in 1960. The places named are located in the Manitoba Interlake region near Lake Manitoba where many Icelanders settled.

VEG

Memorial Fund Contributors

Donations to the memorial funds dedicated to the publishing of this book are gratefully acknowledged herewith:

The Unitarian Universalist Historial Society Fund, Boston, Massachusetts:

R. Glenn and Elaine Argetsinger, St. Louis Park, MN; Ralph and Ann Bennett, Hopkins, MN; Michael R. Carroll, Minneapolis, MN; David H. Cochran, Excelsior, MN; Hellen C. Goudsmit, Minneapolis, MN; Howard F. Huelster, St. Paul, MN; Paulette Y. Johnston, Bloomington, MN; Albert L. Lehman, Minnetonka, MN; Neal and Sharon Lockwood, Wayzata, MN; Gary R. Macomber, Hopkins, MN; Kilian P. Molitor, Robbinsdale, MN; Desyl L. Peterson, Maple Plain, MN; Roy D. Phillips, St. Paul, MN; Daniel Quillin and Marg Hinz-Quillin, Minneapolis, MN; Robert A. Saugen, Minneapolis, MN; and John E. Thomas, Excelsior, MN.

The Emil Gudmundson Book Fund, Winnipeg, Manitoba:

Rannveig and Leslie Gudmundson, Lundar, MB; Gudny and Geiri Eiriksson, Lundar, MB; James Goodman, Flin Flon, MB; Mrs. Pat Crocker, Charleswood, MB; Arborg Federated Ladies Aid, Arborg, MB; Steinunn and Miss Johnson, Lundar, MB; Arnold and Patsy Kirby and family, Lundar, MB; Margaret and Eric Bjornson, Winnipeg, MB; Mrs. Annie Johnson, Vogar, MB; Stefan Jonasson, Winnipeg, MB; Miss Eleanor Cook, Winnipeg, MB; Palmi Palsson, Arborg, MB; Einar and Vordis Oddleifson, Arborg, MB; Mrs. Laufey Harris, Lundar, MB; Mrs. Gudrun Eyjolfson, Lundar, MB; Gudni and Gunna Myrdal, Lundar, MB; Mrs. Laufey Gudmundson, Winnipeg, MB; Helen and Robert Nation, Winnipeg, MB; Mrs. Thorbjorg Davidson, Winnipeg, MB; Ladies Aid of the Unitarian Church of Winnipeg, Winnipeg, MB; Mrs. Elinborg Olson, Winnipeg, MB; Miss Margret Petursson, Winnipeg, MB; Gustaf Kristjanson, Winnipeg, MB; Arborg Unitarian Church, Arborg, MB; Veiga Gudmundson, Wynyard, SK; Susan Havdal, Duluth, MN; Edith Sunley, Manhasset, NY; Franklin and Dora Sigurdson, Winnipeg, MB; Helga Olafson, Vancouver, BC; Valdi Bjornsson, Lundar, MB; Steve and Lara Arnason, Lundar, MB; Gimli Unitarian Church, Gimli, MB; and Helgi Palsson, Arborg, MB.

The Memorial Fund for Emil Gudmundson, Minneapolis-St. Paul, Minnesota:

State Rep. Wesley and Linda Skoglund, Minneapolis, MN; Dr. Donald and Elizabeth Wheeler, Minneapolis, MN; Patricia and Daniel Amborn, Luverne, MN; Agnes and Russell Amlee, Bloomington, MN; Elaine and Glenn Argetsinger, St. Louis Park, MN; Ralph and Ann Bennett, Hopkins, MN; Doris and Michael Bialas, Chicago, IL; Gladys Bakken, Hanska, MN; Ella Bjorneberg, Madelia, MN; Clara, Lorraine and Ardelle Becken, Hanska, MN; Algor and Bonita Blomquist, Hanska, MN; Allan and Nancy Carlson, Bloomington, MN; Mr. and Mrs. Kenneth Chambard, Sandstone, MN; Michael R. Carroll, Minneapolis, MN; Norma J. Cudd, Minneapolis, MN; Lee and Muriel Fredrickson, Hanska, MN; David H. Cochran, Greenwood, MN; Joan Miller; Hellen and Arnoldus Goudsmit, Minneapolis, MN; Judy Hamilton, St. Paul, MN; Oscar and Maynard Moe; Inga Ostlund, Hanska, MN; Rikka Hanson, Madelia, MN; Wallace and Joyce Hetle, Hanska, MN; Benjamin Jr. and Margery Pease, Boise, ID; Alvin Shelley, Hanska, MN; John E. and Signe J. Thomas, Excelsior, MN; Dora Gunlaugson Stowe, Richfied, MN; Frances Gunlaugson, Richfied, MN; Glyndon and Beverly Webb, St. Cloud, MN; Robert Saugen, Minneapolis, MN; Clarise and Ezra Sandman, St. James, MN; Desyl L. Peterson, Maple Plain, MN; Clint and Ede Haroldson, Renville, MN; Mary Hinz-Quillin, Minneapolis, MN; Dan Quillin, Minneapolis, MN; Armand and Karlie Jahnke, Minneapolis, MN; Rev. Roy Phillips, St. Paul, MN; Paulette Johnston, Bloomington, MN; Albert L. Lehman, Minnetonka, MN; Dr. Ellsworth Rieke, Taylor Falls, MN; Louise M. Roth, Mankato, MN; Neal and Sharon Lockwood, Wayzata, MN; Pete and Marie Rusten, Hanska, MN; and Gary Macomber, Hopkins, MN.

Chapter 1

The Soil of Icelandic Religious Liberalism

The lead question is: What are the reasons for Icelandic immigrants nearly a century ago being interested in liberal religion and Unitarianism in particular? It is much too vague an answer to respond that theirs is a very literary as well as literate heritage, although this would be a factor. We must ask about the particular conditions in Iceland during the latter half of the nineteenth century that made these settlers prime candidates for liberal religion.

The island people of Iceland had a golden literary age during the twelfth, thirteenth, and fourteenth centuries, when Icelanders produced not only the Sagas about the early settlements of Iceland and Greenland and the lives and accomplishments of the Norse Kings, but also contemporary history, romances of chivalry, epic poetry, and the beginnings of its great religious literature. The 'rímur', a type of skaldic four-line poetry, began to appear at this time. The country enjoyed relative independence and well-being.

The story was a bit different by the end of the fourteenth century. The famous volcano, Hekla, erupted three times, wreaking much havoc. Epidemics raged. The weather was bad, and other natural disasters abounded. Commerce deteriorated and Iceland became subject to foreign domination not too sympathetic either to the culture or to the independence of the people. These oppressive conditions prevailed for 400 years, inhibiting both the material and the spiritual growth of the nation. This can be deduced from a graphic population statistic from the period:

> In 1100 A.D. Iceland is believed to have had a population of 70,000. In the following six centuries the population actually halved. [1]

An upturn did not begin in earnest until about the beginning of the nineteenth century; yet the memory of the culture once enjoyed had not died. Here and there, especially in religion, the literary tradition had endured. With an upturn in population, and an increase in its commercial self-sufficiency, Iceland once again began to return to its literary traditions and even enjoy a literary renaissance. Icelanders went to Copenhagen for an education, and both there and at home organized Literary Societies and periodicals reflecting this renaissance. With the exposure in Copenhagen, the winds of European literature and culture, especially German, were felt. The Icelandic scholar, Stefán Einarsson refers to this period (1750-1830) as the Enlightenment or Neo-Classic period and notes:

> During the 18th century, especially its second half, the scientific, literalistic and rationalistic spirit ultimately derivable from Newton, Locke, Montesquieu, and Voltaire began to filter through to Iceland. [2]

It is, however, the next period from about 1830-75 that gives us some clues as to the trends of thought that characterized a good many of the Icelanders who were to migrate to North America. It was a period of Romanticism which was nationalistic and was expressed both in literature and in politics. The leading writers, who often resided in Copenhagen, were influenced by the political and cultural outlooks present in the revolutions of France and Germany. They were not unaware of the spirit of freedom and independence that was gaining ground widely in Europe at the time. The most notable leader among the Icelanders of this period was Jón Sigurðsson who was outstanding as a philologist and historian, but is now long remembered as a statesman and political genius who led the nation to a degree of independence it had not had for six centuries. The Republic of Iceland memorializes Sigurðsson by observing their Celebration of Independence on his birthdate, June 17.

These stirrings, which were both literary and political, hastened the day of partial independence or home rule. It occurred in August 1874, one thousand years after the establishment of the first Althing (Parliament) at Thingvellir. The patriots of the day were more often than not also the leading poets and writers. One of them, the Rev. Matthías Jochumsson, wrote Iceland's national hymn for the occasion. [3]

Despite national disasters such as the volcanoes of the 1870's and abnormally cold weather, Iceland was again on its cultural and literary feet, only to be faced with losing almost 25% of its population through emigration to the New World in the last quarter of the nineteenth century. The Icelandic immigrants brought to North America the vibrancy and enthusiasm of this new renaissance which was a curious blend of romanticism and independence, of socialism and individualism, of religion and rationalism, of poetry and politics. A great many of them lived comfortably in two worlds — the literary, cultural, and historical perspectives of the old country, and also the political and vocational realities of the new, to which they soon adapted.

Any assessment of the Icelandic "cultural soil" which primed many Icelanders for Unitarianism, must note that from its earliest years Icelandic Christianity adapted itself to the old pagan Norse ways and legends and myths, and never totally succeeded in replacing them. Even the Reformation had its own unique flavor in Iceland ranging from the pure orthodox Christian Passion poetry of Hallgrímur Pétursson to the oral traditions in verse and folk tales that kept alive the legends that had their roots in Norse mythology.

This accommodation of Christianity to the old myths and practices produced considerable diversity within the church in Iceland over the centuries, even when on the surface it bowed to

orthodox strictures. There was no official religious toleration in
Iceland until late in the nineteenth century; yet tolerance was
practiced in varying degrees throughout the country. Such was
the case at the time of the greatest emigration to the New
World. The myths, legends, and practices of the past were most
often associated with the topography, geography, and climate
of this rugged island, and for many the rocks, cliffs, and valleys
were the living abodes of these legends. When the emigrants
arrived in the New World with vastly different topography and
geography, the old myths and superstitions were often dropped
and replaced with either a purer and more orthodox
Christianity or Lutheranism, or with a new Rationalism. 4

Tensions and conflicts were not uncommon among church
leaders in Iceland in the period 1870 — 1900, even as a great
deal of latitude and authority was given to each individual
parish and clergyman. Religious tolerance could exist in some
parishes such as Reykjavík and Akureyri while it was in short
ration elsewhere. An incident from the turn of the century
makes this clear. A prominent farmer and chairman of the
township board near Seyðisfjörður died at a relatively early
age. Being an avowed Unitarian, having been an early member
in the 1890's of the Winnipeg church, he had requested that the
burial would take place without reference to the Trinity. The
pastor of the parish refused burial in the church cemetery.
When the widow, also a Unitarian, persisted and laid the body
to rest in unhallowed ground on their farm, the pastor brought
suit against her for violating both the health and religious laws
of the country. The widow fought the case and finally got the
ear of the King of Denmark*, who sided with her.
Subsequently the highest court of the country ruled in her
favor, making a landmark decision for religious toleration and
freedom. 5

The religious toleration in Iceland, as in many countries with
State churches, is rooted in different assumptions, and
subsequently has a different flavor than is found in either the
United States or Canada. In Iceland even to this day, all
individuals are "born into the State church", and church
baptism is the official method of naming a child and recording

---

*At the time Iceland and Denmark shared the same constitutional monarch.

births. Those who seek an alternative, such as belonging to another religious faith, or belonging to no church, must publicly resign from the church. In contrast, in the United States and Canada the state assumes that one is born "without a church" and that the act of church affiliation is a conscious one on the part of either the parents or the individual. This difference was to be a heady experience for many Icelanders in North America, but the traditions and the climate of the old country had prepared many for the change.

1. Sigurður A. Magnússon **Northern Sphinx: Iceland and the Icelanders from the Settlement to the Present.** Montreal: McGill Queens University Press, 1977. p. 117.

2. Stefán Einarsson **A History of Icelandic Literature** New York: The John Hopkins Press, 1957.

3. Matthías Jochumsson translated several English hymns into Icelandic and one can presume that he was quite familiar with the English Unitarian hymnody of the latter half of the 19th century. In the style of the day many of his original hymns as well as the ones he chose to translate are romantic and confident songs of praise, sometimes bordering on sentimentalism. His poem, still sung as the Icelandic National Anthem, (Our Nation's God) **Ó Guð vors Lands** is representative. The second verse, freely translated by the late Rev. Albert E. Kristjánsson is a good specimen of this type of poetry by Jochumsson:

> O Lord of Life, we lean on Thee
> Our Life's but a storm-tossed and quivering reed.
> We perish if Thou art not light of our Life,
> And we lean on Thy strength in our need.
> Be Thou each morning the light that we love,
> Our Leader and Guide through the day,
> Our Comfort at Night sending calm from above
> And the Captain the nations obey.
> May the year probing Love's own triumph song
> While we follow the gleam that the faithful have seen
> Through the fullness of Thy Kingdom's day.

4. The author grew up in a community where a Lutheran minister was named Adam and he and his wife named six of their seven children with old Norse names: Hrund, Freyr, Sif, Thor and Bragi an indication of this very strong Norse influence.

5. Two essays tell this story in detail:

Halldór Stefánsson, **Frikírkjuhreyfing í Dvergasteinsprestakalli** in **Múlaþing.** (Free church Movement in the parish of Dvergasteinn)

Jón Helgason, **Leiðið á Hánefsstaðaeyrum** a chapter in his book **Íslenzkt Mannlíf.** Reykjavik. ("The Grave at Hánefsstaðir")

(Ielandic Daily Life) The weekly newspaper, **Bjarki,** published at Seyðisfjörður in 1901-02 gave accounts of these events as they occurred.

VEG

Chapter 2

The Soul of Icelandic Religious Liberalism — Magnús Eiríksson

Magnús Eiríksson (1806-1881) is the most original of all Icelandic liberal religionists and scholars. He spent his entire career in Denmark, and most of his writings are in Danish, some 18 books mostly on theological topics. Although he never attained any position of prominence either at the University or in the church, his works seem to have been known by his contemporaries both in Denmark and in Iceland. Dr. Águst H. Bjarnason, a professor of philosophy at the University of Iceland for some 30 years (1910-1940), called Eiríksson the "First Icelandic Unitarian" in a lecture he delivered at both Harvard Divinity School and the Meadville Theological School in 1923. [1]

Magnús Eiríksson born 1806 in a rather remote area of northeastern Iceland, was reared by a sensitive stepfather and a mother who had ambitions for her son. Despite the poverty of the home, he received more than the usual tutoring, and at age 18 he enrolled at the Academy at Bessastaðir, graduating five years later at the head of his class. He had hoped to continue his education in theology in Copenhagen, but poverty postponed this dream. Instead he took a position as a clerk for the governor, Mr. Krieger, who became sufficiently impressed with Eiríksson that he became his benefactor, enabling him to fulfill his dream. In 1831 he sailed for Copenhagen, enrolled in theology, and six years later graduated with distinction. He considered a parish in Iceland upon graduation, but as his interest was in further pursuing his scholarly interests, he remained in Copenhagen. He had a great interest and skill in Biblical exegesis while at the Univerisity. This never waned, and in time became the basis for his theological point of view.

Denmark's intellectual climate of the time was rich and vigorous, especialy in religion and theology. This was the period of the three giants in theology: Grundtvig (1783-1872), Martensen (1808-1884), and Kierkegaard (1813-1855). Bjarnason has a somewhat oversimplified but nevertheless useful typology for the core philosophy of these three thinkers as well as Eiríksson:

> Grundtvig — Credo quia revelation (I believe because it is revealed)
>
> Martensen — Credo ut intelligam (I believe in order to understand)
>
> Kierkegaard — Credo quia absurdum (I believe because it is absurd)
>
> Eiríksson — Intelligo ut credum (I understand in order to believe) 2

Eiríksson never received a teaching appointment, but rather was for some time a popular tutor, allowing him an adequate income and time to pursue his own independent studies. He was interested mainly in Biblical and exegetical scholarship, but in addition had a passion for some of the issues of the day. He became embroiled in a controversy over the religious freedom of a small group of Baptists in Denmark, especially their right not to have their children baptized as infants. The ecclesiastical authorities persecuted this small sect; the secular authorities fined them; bishops and professors rationalized these actions theologically. Eiríksson came to the defense of the Baptists. In 1844 he privately published a small book, called **Baptists and Baptism,** in which he not only argued for religious freedom, but sought to prove that Scripture justified adult baptism. On the issue of religious liberty he was articulate:

> When the church in order to be Christian
> transgresses and annihilates as much as it can the
> Law of Charity which is the very essence and
> foundation of Christian faith, then I say, it
> manifestly works its own destruction as a Christian
> commonweal; and the more it has been capable of
> establishing the principle of intolerance and
> unfriendliness, the more it has already proven it is
> not a Christian commonweal except in name...3

He continued writing and publishing in a similar vein for the next five years, and published six books, three of them attacks on the Hegelianism of Martensen, always taking a rationalist position in the interpretation of Scripture.

Magnús Eiríksson although first a theologian, was also an ethicist and a Christian reformer, never recoiling from taking a stand on controversial issues. In his early years in Denmark he was one of a group of Icelandic students whose strong spirit of independence and yen for freedom was accompanied by writings and oratory that reawakened the Icelandic nation. For him the love of Christ must operate both in the life of an individual and in the fabric of society.4

His was no parochial mind, for he sided with those Danes who sought greater participation in the affairs of state, the only Icelander to take an active part in what was known as the "Hippodrome movement" seeking an elected legislature and freedom of religion. According to his major biographer, Eiríkur Albertsson, he loved the Danish nation with a passion even while he was severely critical of Danish policies and authorities in regard to Iceland.

Other issues had Eiríksson's attention but none more than the rights of women:

> The chief problem women have is that they have not
> been able to use or show the spiritual strengths that
> lie in their souls. Up to this time they have been
> given a defined and limited stall in which they could
> only do household duties, with only men having the
> opportunity to exert their potential in a wide and
> free area both as individuals and in public.5

Eiríksson does not have any doubts about the abilities of women, and in particular believes that their natural inclinations lean toward medicine and healing, and he points out that in the old Norse literature both before and after the introduction of Christianity, it was commonly said of a woman, "She was a good physician".

His arguments were written in the form of letters to a contemporary feminist, Clara Raphael, and published under a pseudonym, Theodor Immanuel. In these he seems to have anticipated the arguments of John Stuart Mill some twenty years later in his lengthy and definitive work, **Slavery of Women**. As in the case of other controversies in which he was engaged, Eiríksson took his positions from his theology. When he argued for social justice he based his arguments upon theological premises such as the unity of God. 6

> There was a mental kinship between Clara Raphael and Theodor Immanuel and therefore no wonder that he already in his second letter addresses her as his sister. Their religious conceptions were very much akin. Miss Raphael had in her letters had a great deal to remark about baptism, original sin, the Atonement, the Trinity, and the Divinity of Christ. Her relation to God was a childlike confidence in Him and her confession was as follows: 'I have never before had the feeling that there was any need for a mediator between God and me....There is one God, the Father of us all; I cannot think that he is divided into three. I believe in the Holy Unity, not in the Holy Trinity.' 7

After this controversy there was a 12-year silence, broken in 1863 with the first of several works on scriptural criticism. He argues in 1863 that the Gospel of John is not a bona fide gospel. It could not have been written by a Palestinian Jew, and certainly not by John the Disciple, but rather by a Gnostic Christian in the middle of the Second Century.

Eiríksson at no time is concerned with sectarian labels, never questions being a Lutheran as such, for he thought of himself first and foremost as a scholar trained to discern the truth.

However, this dedication led him to beliefs that were very unitarian, such as the concept of the unity of God rather than the Trinity, the primary humanity of Jesus, and a rational and critical view of Scripture. There is no indication in his writings that he has any interest in Unitarianism as a movement, but rather he seems influenced by German theologians of the time, especially the Tubingen school. Only in one work, **God and the Reformer** (1863), does he mention a Unitarian, Theodore Parker, but it is as a reformer not as a theologian.

Eiríksson never gained any prominence among his contemporary theological scholars in Denmark, and both ecclesiastical and governmental authorities tried to disgrace him. He had some small influence on a few religious leaders in Sweden, and a few of his works were translated. His ideas and his writings were known in Iceland, and a few like Matthías Jochumsson had great admiration for him and even visited him. On the other hand, many of the Icelandic clergy viewed his ideas with scorn.

In the Icelandic version of his Harvard lecture, Dr. Bjarnason concludes:

> Magnús Eiríksson was rightly named **the apostle of truth** by contemporaries. He died undefeated, and undefeated he will live in the memory of his nation when it has become as pure in faith as he; when it chooses to believe what Christ actually taught, rather than what the church decrees.[8]

1. Agust H Bjarnason. **Magnús Eiríksson, The First Icelandic Unitarian** is an unpublished, handwritten manuscript in Andover Harvard Library at the Harvard Divinity School, Cambridge, MA: The same lecture also appeared in Icelandic in Skirnir, vol. 98

2. Ibid.

3. Ibid. Quoting from Magnús Eiríksson **Om Baptister og Barnedab**, 1844. pp 19-20.

4. Eirikur Albertsson. **Magnús Eiríksson Guðfræð Hans og Trúarlif**, 1938. privately published in Reykjavik, 1938 is the definitive biography of the life and theology of Eiríksson.

5. Ibid, p. 111.

6. Halldór E. Johnson. **Magnús Eiríksson the Reformer** is an essay in Stephen H. Fritchman **Men Of Liberty**, Boston Beacon Press 1947.

7. Bjarnason, see above.

8. Ibid.

Chapter 3

The Heart of Icelandic Religious Liberalism — Matthías Jochumsson and The English Unitarian Influence

The influence of Matthías Jochumsson (1835-1920) upon his fellow countrymen, including those who emigrated, is very clear and direct compared to that of Magnús Eiríksson. For one thing, Jochumsson remained in Iceland, although he made several extended trips abroad to both Denmark and England. He was a literary Romantic in his thought, with his roots deep into the Icelandic traditions — including the religious — on the one hand, and a yearning for new thought and new ideas on the other. He was a prolific writer, both in poetry and prose and early in his career became well-known. He was, like many of his contemporaries, a nationalist and quite naturally wrote a hymn on the occasion of the Millennial Celebration of the Althing in 1874 which to this date is the Icelandic National Anthem. From the succeeding generation to Jón Sigurðsson he was held in esteem second only to that of Sigurðsson by the emigrants.

Matthías Jochumsson was born in the northwest of Iceland in 1835. He was tutored privately as a young man, until his late twenties when he attended the Gymnasium and Theological School in Reykjavik. Early in his ministry he was introduced to the **Works of William Ellery Channing** by a senior pastor in rural Iceland, and was deeply influenced by them. Early in his ministry Jochumsson was twice deeply bereaved by the loss of his first two wives. He reflects in his autobiography "that the rational beliefs of Channing were positive for bereavement." 1

During the second period of bereavement Jochumsson chose to spend a year in England to regain his perspective. He had arranged to stay with the eminent Unitarian scholar and preacher, Dr. James Martineau, but because of Martineau's illness, the plans were changed. Instead he was the guest of the Rev. Robert Spears and his family in London. Mr. Spears was then the General Secretary of the British Unitarian Association and editor of **Christian Life.** It turned out to be a very important eventful period in his life, for not only did he develop a very strong, deep, and lasting friendship with the Spears family, and make an acquaintance with English Unitarianism, but he found his doubts about orthodoxy and his espousal of Channing Unitarianism vindicated. He considered Channing to be 200 years ahead of his time, especially in relation to Biblical studies, for although he rejected the seven thorny points of Calvinism including the Trinity and the deity of Jesus Christ, at the same time he alleged Jesus Christ to be the most holy of God's sons and an example for all mankind.

Jochumsson, undoubtedly a good scholar, nevertheless was always more the poet than the rationalist and the analyst. He responded to ideas and events with an enthusiasm if not a passion. Upon his return to Iceland from his first sojourn in England, he seriously considered starting a Unitarian mission there, and with some financial assistance from the British Unitarian Association published a liberal journal in Reykjavik. But he was first an Icelander, a passionate nationalist, and a Romantic traditionalist which of course included the Lutheran tradition. He was comfortable in promoting his liberal religious views (or modernist as he later called them), but he recoiled from establishing a sect in a country where sects were hardly known. At the time he felt compelled to liberalize the Lutheran State church about which he said in 1878:

> (it) is cold and dead owing its existence only to old
> and outworn laws and traditions ... we want, as it
> were, a new Evangelism: we want a national revival

that summons and joins the scattered members and elements of our nation, we want to raise ourselves for the common work of reformation. 2

All the while Jochumsson was expressing his rationalistic views about religion in his lecturing and prose, he was also writing hymns and poetry which were beloved by all, whether liberal or orthodox. Many of his hymns were translations such as his version of "What a Friend We Have in Jesus". Others were somewhat nationalistic such as the national anthem. The didactic arguments were totally absent, leading a pious and conservative Lutheran pastor in Manitoba to state that it would be desirable to make Jochumsson refrain from utterances in prose and to write only poetry. Jochumsson recognized this "tension" in himself for he states, "I believe with my heart, I doubt with my head." 3

For most of his career, he served State Lutheran churches, the longest tenure being at the prestigious parish at Akureyri. He later narrowly lost his bid in becoming the Dean of the Cathedral in Reykjavik, some think because of his liberal views in theology.

This ambivalence with sectarianism, and the tension between his "heart and head" seems to have been present during his entire ministry. He never retreated from his very strong admiration for Channing and his dedication to "Channing's Christianity". He found the Unitarianism of England of his day too coldly intellectual, and not focused sufficiently upon Christ as the center. Yet in his prolific letter-writing he kept in touch with religious liberals in England and the United States, for his command of English was excellent. In addition to his British contacts, he carried on considerable correspondence with a leading American free thinker, Dr. Paul Carus of La Salle, Illinois and publisher of **The Open Court**. 4 One must almost conclude that he enjoyed dealing, in his correspondence, with liberal ideas which he found hard to accept, but refrained from any personal discussions of them. Jochumsson visited the Chicago Exposition in 1893, at the very time of the World Congress of Religion in which Carus was deeply involved as Secretary. Yet he seems to have made but one small attempt to see Carus; he did not attend the Congress, but visited the Fair with his old Icelandic friends. On this same trip he stopped over in Winnipeg and later in his letters expressed his discomfort with the Unitarians under the leadership of Björn Pétursson confessing to a greater spiritual kinship with the Rev. Jón Bjarnason and the Lutherans.

The legacy remains, however, that Jochumsson had a great influence upon a large portion of the immigrants, and challenged them to question the rigidity of the creeds, the traditions, and the institutions. All the while he spoke to them through his poetry and kindled their passions for their country, their God, and their human Christ. The Icelanders were tremendous readers of poetry, and it was simple to supplement Jochumsson's moderation and sentimentalism in some of his hymns with the reading of the poetry of his contemporaries, Thorsteinn Erlíngson and Steingrímur Thorsteinsson. From it many received their philosophy of life.

1., 2., 3. I presume that these comments are to be found In Jochumsson's autobiographic sketches, **Sögukaflar af Sjálfum Mér.**   GEB
4. **The Open Court** was edited for many years by Paul Carus (1852 — 1919) as a journal devoted to the establishment of religion and ethics on a scientific basis.

Chapter 4

The American "Radical" Link Stephan G. Stephansson

Yea, it is well to understand and know
That it is not a sentient thing, my dear,
With evil for its aim, that struck you so,
But accident upon its chance-career.
No cosmic law, but simple savagery,
Designs and wills the keenest agony.
- Stephan G. Stephansson — **Gestur** (1909)

This verse, a part of a rather long poem, was written in bereavement when the poet and his family faced the brute reality of the untimely death of their sixteen-year old son and brother who was struck by lightning on the farm. These are hardly words of a Romantic trying to explain why bad things happen, nor is it Job's answer of resignation, but rather the words of a Realist who, in consoling himself, cannot even call upon an explanation outside of himself and the Nature of which he is a part.

This is one of but several possible examples of this poet's world view and religious outlook, beginning in the late 1880's and continuing until his death in 1927. He accepted no consistent label, but among those given him are freethinker, atheist, humanist, materialist, and unitarian. None really fully described him, and each had a limited usefulness, but in his poetry, letters, and prose he consistently raised some daring and provocative questions about the issues of the meaning of life and death. He seemed to have an ability to articulate better than the average person a philosophy of life that was not commonplace, yet seemed to find considerable acceptance among fellow immigrants. He worked his way through acceptance of his Lutheran faith, which in America was often quite orthodox, to rather, non-traditional unbeliefs and positions, and influenced many others through his writings and correspondence. He is today hailed as one of the greatest poets of all time to write in the Icelandic language, [1] for his themes and his substance were very universal. At times his themes were related more to the New World of the day than the old, leading one to surmise that he was in thought an American.

Stephen G. Stephansson was born in Iceland in 1853, the son of very poor farmers who possessed keen intelligence, and who were kin of some of the leading men of letters. He had few opportunities for formal education:

> Due to the poverty of my parents, the only books we had were the Bible and a few religious tracts, but I read everything I could lay my hands on, good or bad, depending largely upon the kindness of our neighbors. I became at age 15 a hired man to my uncle and it was my good fortune that he had a well-stocked library of which I took good advantage. [2]

Much later, he reflected that in his youth he considered the Bible divinely inspired.

At age 20 he set sail for the New World, arriving in Milwaukee, and spent the next year as a day laborer. With some money saved, he struck out with a bride to a homestead in Shawano County, Wisconsin. Hardships continued, but he did not give up his habit of reading. On his own he learned the English language, not only to speak it but to read it, and as a testament to this determination, his personal library contains a well worn copy of the **National Fourth Reader**, inscribed on the fly leaf with his name and the date, 7 - 4 - 74. Aso on the fly-leaf is the name of Rasmus B. Anderson the great friend of all Icelanders in Wisconsin. One must assume that he received his copy from Anderson's library. He seemed to adjust well to the New World, continuing his reading. A decade and a half later he wrote to a friend that "One must read; otherwise we become nothing but belly and mouth."

In 1880 he moved to a new and larger Icelandic settlement in Pembina Country, Dakota Territory. Here he found several old friends, among them, a gifted and restless young Lutheran minister, Páll Thorláksson, a graduate of Concordia Seminary in St. Louis and quite orthodox. But he was apparently a stimulating friend, for he was sophisticated and well read. Stephansson joined the Lutheran Church in this new community when it was organized and became its secretary. At once he objected to two articles of the constitution, regarding the confessions and the exclusion of women from the governance of the church. Nevertheless he remained a member and 5 years later was a delegate to the first convention of the Icelandic Lutheran Synod. Here he fared no better on these two issues, and subsequently dropped out of all involvement with the Lutheran Church. He then became one of its most outspoken critics. Stephansson reviews this period much later in a letter to friends in Iceland:

> We, the late Páll Thorláksson the Synod minister, and I were good friends and knew each other well. He knew about my doubts. I was but a young man in his twenties, but not as purely skeptical as now. It was as if Páll tolerated everything in me and sometimes he delivered sermons that were directed at me. For example, one time young men of my age who are now "lights of the Synod" got into an argument with me about the **Book of Revelations** and I said something like this: '**The Book of Revelations** is nothing but a kind of **Battle of the Fields of Death** of early Christendom written by some Gröndal* of the time.' Of course I said this

---

* Benedict Gröndal, (1826 - 1907) wrote an Icelandic mock-heroic novel, **Heljarslóðar Orrusta (The Battle of the Fields of Death)**, in which he satirized the public and military affairs of Europe in the nineteenth century. Although Stephansson's rationale in comparing Gröndal's work with the **Book of Revelations** is not clear, his suggestion that the **Bible** is secular in origin appears significant.

jokingly although I was serious that the book was put together only by humans. Well, next Sunday, the Rev. Mr. Thorláksson, although he was not present at the discussion, preached about the danger that befalls those who question divine revelation, and especially for those who say, for example, that the **Book of Revelations** and the **Battle of the Fields of Death** can be equated. ...

Rev. Thorláksson was then the minister of a Norwegian congregation in Shawano County, Wisconsin, but preached sometimes for us Icelanders where we lived, although we had no congregational organization ourselves.

Rev. Thorláksson organized the first congregation at Garðar, North Dakota. There I was the secretary. Everyone present signed the congregational by-laws and statement of purpose. I read the motion for the vote, and he asked me to let him see it. I obliged. After a while he said it was all in order except that my name and approval as secretary was missing and he asked me to correct it. I refused. He asked for an explanation. I obliged. I stated, as was true, that I alone voted against two articles of the by-laws: the one that dealt with the Confessions and the other which denied women the vote. I said a little about why I disagreed. He did not answer, but asked me whether he could sign the records, if he noted beside my name that for me personally these two articles were not acceptable. I approved. He wrote my name, then read to me what he had written. ... that was my standing in the congregation from then on. After Páll Thorláksson died, the Garðar congregation split. On the surface was the issue of the women's vote. But underneath, there were all kinds of criticism ... and the splinter was really fighting for what is now called modernism or higher criticism, which in essence is the refutation that the Confessions or Scripture are infallible.

> All the Icelandic congregations were called to a Synod convention in Winnipeg in 1885, including our splinter in Garðar with two delegates. I accepted election at the behest of my fellow members, although the clergy and the leading laymen of our neighboring congregations opposed us. Because of my friends, I did not want to be absent if controversy arose. Such is my Christianity. Our congregation was not rebuked. I was even nominated for vice-chairman, then secretary, but I categorically refused.
>
> I was then elected the vice-secretary. I stated the obvious: that I was too lazy to refuse such a meaningless office . . . . I did not attend the next convention for I had nothing to report. The Garðar congregation was the only one to recognize women. ... I was out of the congregation when the next Convention was held. And I have not been a member of any congregation since then.[3]

Stephansson's interest in religious values and ethics did not stop with his rejection of the Lutheran congregation at Garðar. He found others in the settlement who shared his views about traditional religion, finding its doctrines especially discouraging to free inquiry. In the middle of the winter of 1888 he and others gathered at his home to organize The Icelandic Cultural Society. He wrote and account of this meeting in the Icelandic Winnipeg weekly, **Lögberg:**

> ### HUMANITY, RESEARCH, FREEDOM
> The objectives of this organization are to support and promote culture and ethics, that ethics and that faith which is based upon experience, knowledge and science. In place of ecclesiastical sectarianism, it seeks humanitarianism and fellowship; in place of unexamined confessions of faith, sensible and unfettered research; in place of blind faith, independent conviction; and in place of ignorance

and superstition, spiritual freedom and progress
upon which no fetters are placed. 4

These are the words of the preamble of this new
organization, and then Stephansson continues with
commentary:

> This society was organized last February 4th (1888)
> by seven men. It was the opinion of the charter
> members that most organizations either enslave
> men to ancient ideas or attempt to erect narrow
> limits for study and thinking and are not capable of
> meeting today's greatest need which is free inquiry
> and self-education. The ideas of those who join the
> Society are never dictated by the members, however
> few may belong, for its objective is to give mutual
> support and encouragement for each member to
> become better informed and morally stronger
> without any restriction as to what any person may
> accept or reject. It is expected that the membership
> will divide into groups which shall each take
> different and specific areas of inquiry, and especially
> those which concern the commonweal. These types
> of societies have been established in several places in
> this country, and have prospered, though they are
> relatively new and small numerically. Professor
> Felix Adler of New York is the founder. 5

The Society prospered for the next two or three years.
Stephansson was the secretary and kept detailed records. The
by-laws are relatively simple. Thirty-four names are listed in the
membership rolls, among them two men who were to touch the
early Unitarian story quite closely: Björn Pétursson missionary
and founder of the Icelandic Unitarian Church of Winnipeg
and Skapti Brynjólfsson, a North Dakota State Senator who
later became the third president of the Winnipeg Church.
Members took turns in the preparation of papers on such
topics as Natural History, Comparative Religions and
Mythology, and the History of Religions. Guest speakers were
occasionally featured, and Pétursson, for instance, spoke on

Unitarianism, and Stephansson gave a public lecture on the thought of Robert Ingersoll. The Society also established a modest library and some of the recorded titles were: **Bible Myths, Kingdoms in Nature, Childhood Man, Childhood of Religions; and North American Review.**

When word of this Society reached some of the leaders in the Icelandic settlements in North Dakota and Manitoba, the reception was mixed. Even before Stephansson's news item about its founding appeared in **Lögberg,** the periodical of the Icelandic Lutheran Synod, **Sameining,** had a rather unflattering news item about the organization that began:

> That spirit exists that holds that Sunday Schools are the worst and most dangerous of institutions for youth, for they learn nothing but lifeless banalities namely the Biblical Word of God which is the greatest poison for society, and an impediment to all culture and freedom as well as all science and progress, and keeps people in oppression and ignorance. 6

Such was the opening blast towards this new Cultural Society. The author is not named, but scholars surmise that it was the Synod's minister in Pembina County, the Rev. F.J. Bergmann. The editor of **Sameining**, Rev. Jón Bjarnason, assures his readers that this letter bears the truth, and cannot refrain from adding that:

> one should not overlook that this society has been organized by uneducated Icelandic farmers who have attained such arrogance here in America that they consider themselves competent to challenge the Christian Church, the greatest institution of all time. 7

In the following issue, Bjarnason continues the attack in a lengthy editorial. First he attacks the concept and reality of religious freedom in American, for with it comes the freedom to disbelieve. In contrast, he notes that in Iceland any free-thought ideas would have to be individually held, seldom publicly uttered, and certainly never the basis for any organization. The clear implication is that these men are being more than unchristian; they are unfaithful to their Icelandic heritage:

> Though **Sameining** knows that just as men are Christian in Iceland, they can be unChristian in America, and although there are many excellent aspects to American culture and society, we see in light of this, no reason to urge people, directly or indirectly to emigrate. [8]

Stephansson took pen to hand and responded in a lengthy rebuttal in **Lögberg.** It is obvious, he states, that the writer cannot know anything about the Society first hand, for he lays charges on the Society with events and opinions that were expressed in a public debate with which the Society had no connection. He sees the **Sameining** attack as three-fold: the charge that the Cultural Society is a free-thought society; the charge that the Society holds a single opinion on creeds or religious beliefs; and the charge that the members who are beginning to have doubts have their original anti-Christian stance and are about to recant. He answers these one by one. To the first he asks whether it is heretical to believe that one should follow those beliefs and morals that experience and the knowledge from good and wise men have agreed will bring happiness to humanity here on earth. If so, then the Society is a free-thought society. To the second he points out that the Society has taken no stands on **Sameining** or the Church, for the personal beliefs of its members vary greatly. Thus any position would be an individual one, and he does acknowledge that the statements referred to in **Sameining** actually were uttered in a public debate about the time the Society was organized. And to the last charge he asserts that the Society has not changed a word in its Statement of Purpose, and furthermore does not acknowledge that it is anti-Christian. Then Stephansson jumps to the attack rather sarcastically:

> There is something rather funny about **Sameining's** description of "free thinking that continued to swim in the deep." I am of course no fisherman and

besides I have never heard of such a beast. If **Sameining** has reference to free thinking individuals, then it is natural they proceed slowly. First and foremost, it should not be surprising that men do not change their opinions that have been inculcated through long and serious consideration, for it is infrequent that what later will appear to be Truth is revealed to men all at once, and undoubtedly some will shrink from being the brunt of attacks such as **Sameining** has made on the Cultural Society. When all is said and done, then the Cultural Society must consider it its good luck that **Sameining** took the position it did. When some time passes and men's thoughts have been calmed, then one might take a little closer look at this, and the articles in **Sameining** will be evidence of the general direction and the caliber of leadership of the Icelandic Lutheran Synod. 9

The Rev. Jón Bjarnason, the editor of **Sameining** , had the last word in this public debate in the August issue where he asserts that the Icelandic Cultural Society is truly a free-thinkers' society, and then he attacks Stephansson personally:

Mr. Stefán Guðmundsson was a delegate to the first Synod Convention in 1885, accepted its articles and by-laws and constitution and with it all the Confessions and principles of our Lutheran Christian faith, and accepted election as the vice-secretary of the Synod. Later he dropped out of his own congregation silently, and obviously out of the Synod and nothing more was heard of him until this 'Cultural Spirit' enters him and thrusts him upon the scene with this new name: Stephan G. Stephansson.* .....
I will not speak to a dead Free Thinkers Society. 10

*It is noteworthy that Stephan G. Stephansson and Stefán Guðmundsson are one and the same man. He was christened as Stefán, and originally known as Guðmundsson according to the Icelandic patronymic system, his father being named Guðmundur. Guðmundur's father, hence Stefán's grandfather, was named Stefán. In the self-initiated name-change the initial "G" stands for "Guðmundsson" while "Stephan" and "Stephansson" are anglicizations in spelling. The revised name means: Stephan son of Guðmundur who was the son of Stephan.

Stephansson never answered this attack, but the controversy had its effects, one of which was to bring an open debate at the 1888 Synod Convention in Mountain, N.D. on the topic, "Is the Christian Church for or against Free Research." The debate and its arguments are covered more fully in a later chapter on Björn Pétursson.

Very few Icelanders in the New World could have missed this controversy, for it took place in the publications which everyone read, and made the ground more fertile for the development of an Icelandic Unitarian movement. Actually the efforts of the Icelandic Cultural Society were short-lived, for it disbanded in 1893, without any new groups having been organized in other settlements. Many of the leading members moved away from North Dakota, among them Stephansson who resettled in the foothills of the Canadian Rockies, eighty miles north of Calgary. Others moved to Winnipeg, to Seattle, or with Stephansson to Alberta. Yet in this short period, through debates and controversy, the Society had made a great impact on many Icelanders. One of them, Björn Pétursson, organized for the Unitarians in North Dakota and Winnipeg. Others were more low-key but nonetheless had influence.

Many scholars who have studied Stephansson's writings, both poetry and prose, have speculated about the major influences which led him to take a free-though position after presumably being active in the Lutheran Synod. Profs. Watson Kirkconnell [11] and Sigurdur Nordal [12], both eminent and competent scholars, are mindful of his Icelandic roots and his farm experience in Alberta. Sverrir Kristjansson [13] identifies his world view and religious philosophy as Humanist both in the more classical sense and in its 20th century sense. Óskar Halldórsson [14] is probably the most perceptive in noting that Stephansson makes references in his articles and letters to Felix Adler and Robert Ingersoll and pursues this connection. But anyone who is not quite conversant and knowledgeable about American cultural and religious trends of the latter part of the 19 th century would have difficulty discerning the references he makes, and the subtleties in these references. The sometimes subtle references are of greatest interesy in understanding Stephansson's role in the beginnings of liberal religion/Unitarianism among Icelanders in North America.

Stephansson came as a lad of twenty to Milwaukee in 1873 without possessions, with very little formal education and little if any knowledge of the English language. Undoubtedly, it is in character to expect that he soon tried to learn to read as well as speak the English language. The best evidence of this is the **National Fourth Reader**, which has many essays and poems of great quality. Certainly by the mid 1880's Stephansson had a good command of English. We do not know how he made contact with some of the intellectual, radical, and freethought literature of this period, but it was from this source that he secured the books which were part of the Cultural Society's library. He was a poor farmer when he left North Dakota for Alberta, with limited possessions, and one must assume that he would take with him only his prized possessions. Among these are a few volumes which are to be found in his personal library. Of most significance is **The Index**. the weekly publication of the Free Religious Association edited by William J. Potter and B.F. Underwood, for the years 1884 to its cessation in 1886.

It was of such value to him that he had it bound!

So it is that a poor immigrant farmer in North Dakota made contact with a stimulating new and somewhat radical and controversial intellectual movement in the United States. In a letter to a friend in 1890 Stephansson listed nine free-thought publications 15 and evaluated them. He states there that the best book he ever read was **The Debates and Essays of B.F. Underwood.** 16 It should be further noted that Felix Adler, whom he mentions in his news item 17 about the Icelandic Cultural Society was President of the Free Religious Association from 1878 to 1882, and was a frequent contributor to **The Index** even after that.

A little background into the Free Religious Association is needed:

The distinctive thought of late nineteenth-century America was humanistic in character .... The humanistic outlook with its emphasis on man as the central and creative factor in the drama of life, wedded to the sharpened sense of his place in history, largely governed prevailing attitudes toward the new historical sciences of geology and evolutionary biology. [18]

The Free Religious Association, a part of the post-Civil War ferment in the United States, was organized on May 30, 1867 in Boston by persons of differing backgrounds. Many of them were Unitarian clergy and laity, discouraged by what they considered to be the rather narrow Christian viewpoint of the leadership in Boston Unitarianism of the period. The first purpose of the FRA was to promote the interest of pure religion,to encourage the scientific study of religon, and to increase fellowship in the spirit. A second purpose states that every member is responsible for his own opinions. Very early the FRA had within its membership theists and non-theists alike.

The parallel here between the FRA and the Icelandic Cultural Society is so striking that it cannot be an accident, and one must assume that Stephansson had read **The Index** and other of their writings carefully. He also indicates, for instance, in a letter written in 1891 that he was familiar with the personalities of the FRA, when he makes reference to "old man Abbot". This has to be an early FRA leader and Unitarian minister, Francis Ellingwood Abbot. Although he does not quote Abbot, one would assume that Abbot's definition of religion would have an appeal for Stephansson:

> "Religion is not mere thinking or feeling or mere doing, not mere belief or mere sentiment or mere action, but LIVING UPWARD, which is all of them in one"; it is striving to achieve knowledge, love, and virtue. It is "man's obedience to that something within him which ever impels him upward to the better." "It is the soul's deep resolve to love the truth, to learn the truth, and to live the truth, uncoerced and free." It affirms the right to think; the rights of conscience; that a higher law exists; that universal law and transcendent love are identical. [19]

In 1885 the FRA revised its by-laws, including its statement of objectives, in which one finds striking similarities with the Statement of Purpose of the Icelandic Cultural Society:

> The objectives of this Association are to encourage the scientific study of religion and ethics, to advocate freedom in religion, to increase fellowship in the spirit, and to emphasize the supremacy of practical morality in all relations of life. [20]

Stephansson also in his commentaries about the beginnings of the Icelandic Cultural Society refers to "similar organizations that exist around the country", and gives credit in this case to Professor Felix Adler. If this is indeed the case, then he is referring specifically to the Ethical Culture Societies which had been organized in a number of cities at that time. But since he was reading **The Index**, he was undoubtedly also aware of other similar groups that were being organized in various communities around the country including the Midwest. These were called by various names such as the Radical, Liberal, or Free Religious Clubs. These had a bond with the FRA for they were motivated by the same spirit of free inquiry. According to Persons:

> The unanimity with which their constitutions emphasized the importance of free discussion and investigation indicated the widespread feeling at the time that the churches were hostile or indifferent to the current problems that occupied men's minds. They proposed to deal impartially with scientific and moral as well as with religious questions. They were motivated by the desire to establish the authority of reason and right through the search for truth in the scientific spirit. And most of them dedicated themselves to social reform in the interest of progress and equal rights. [21]

By 1876 a national Liberal League organization came into being which brought together some 32 or more local Leagues. Stephansson had these also as models for the Cultural Society. Among the characteristics of the FRA and most of these radical groups of this period were, on the one hand, a spirit of radical individualism, and on the other hand a desire to organize into groups in order to be more effective. The spirit of individualism in most cases prevailed, the Ethical Cultural Societies founded by Adler being the exceptions. But as an intellectual movement, the FRA and others had a great effect upon individuals and upon the American cultural scene. This indeed was also the case with the Icelandic Cultural Society. Though shortlived, its influence among the Icelandic settlers was very great.

As for Stephansson, he was first and always an individualist, and after his involvement in organizing the Icelandic Cultural Society in 1888, remained for the rest of his life rather aloof from organizations of any kind, and certainly religious groups. His sympathies were always liberal, if not radical. His was no run-of-the-mill mind; it was able to comprehend the depth and message of one of the most vibrant, profound, and radical of American cultural and religious movements in the latter half of the 19th century. He was able to transmit the excitement of this movement to his fellow countrymen and women who were living in the United States and Canada. After his involvement with the Cultural Society, Stephanson turned almost exclusively to writing to transmit his views and ideas, and his poetry, letters and essays appeared with some frequency in the Icelandic weeklies in Winnipeg. A great poet he did become, and in his poetry he expressed his religious and social philosophy.

Stephansson, the Poet

Stephansson's contribution to liberal religious thought among the Icelanders would have been great even if it had been restricted to the Icelandic Cultural Society. Always the individualist, he never joined a Unitarian church, but his ideas and his outlook on life, as well as his concern for the commonweal, were to find expression in poetry which he wrote primarily in his Alberta farm home at night after the work of the fields and the stables had been completed.

It is difficult to speak of the poetry of Stephan G. Stephansson without using superlatives. Professor Watson Kirkconnell of the University of Toronto has called him Canada's leading poet.

Professor Frank S. Cawley of Harvard University considered him "the greatest poet of the western world." .... There can be no doubt that Stephan G. Stephansson has enriched Icelandic literature immeasurably and deserves therefore to be ranked with the greatest poets Iceland has produced. When one considers that Stephansson had practically no formal schooling, was a farmer all his life, was a pioneer three times, raised a large family, and was able to study and compose only after wresting a living as a day-laborer or farmer at the expense of sleepless nights, his energy and genius are the more surprising. ... The creative urge was so strong within him that fatigue and occasionally even gaunt hunger were forgotten as he sat alone reading, thinking, and composing. When he finally collected his poems, he published them under the title **Andvökur,** meaning "sleepless or restless nights." 22

Much has been made of the strong influence that his native Iceland had on him, for his poetry is filled with allusions to the Sagas of old, to the traditions of the country, and to its scenery and landscape. He also wrote in the Icelandic poetic traditions with richness of diction and alliteration and in a style which was very Icelandic, although he was also in some ways very original. But the matter of content and ideas can be better understood if one is informed by knowledge of the radical thinking in religious and political circles in the United States during the latter part of the 19th century, and especially an acquaintanceship with the Free Religious movement. An individualist, he never rejoined any church but had an affinity to Unitarianism, and in fact willed that a Unitarian service be used for his funeral. 23

This aspect of the influence upon Stephansson and his writings has yet to be studied thoroughly, but a good start has been made by a scholar at the University of Iceland, Óskar O. Halldórsson. In a dissertation on one of Stephansson's early collections of poems, he explores the apparent affinity he had for the ideas of Felix Adler, and draws some parallels, using quotations from Adler's **Creed and Deed**. It is worth noting some of the examples used. The translations used, of Stephansson's poems, are quite accurate but their original vigor is somewhat lost in the process:

ADLER

Attitude Towards Life:
The dead are not dead, if we have
loved them truly. In our own lives we
give them immortality. .... All the
good that was in them lives in you,
the germ and the nucleus of the
better that shall be.
   — **Creed and Deed,** page 35, 1894
      ed.

Heaven is on this Earth
And now the new Ideal differs from
Christianity in this, that it seeks to
approach the goal of a Kingdom of
Heaven upon earth, not by the
miraculous interference of the Deity,
but by the laborious exertion of men,
and the slow but certain progress of
certain generations.
   — **Creed and Deed,** page 96

Attitude Toward Christ
It was the humanity, not the dogma
of Jesus, by which Christianity
triumphed.
   — **Creed and Deed,** page 163

Progress:
Far from being exemplary, the ideas
of right and wrong entertained by
our earliest progenitors were
infinitely below our own ... Each age
added its own to the stock of virtue,
each contributed its share to swell
the treasure of mankind.
   — **Creed and Deed,** page 73 - 74

STEPHANSSON

The kindness never will be spoiled or
spent;
The spool of time will keep the
thread intact.
Though visions for thy glory with
thee went,
The ones you gave inspired so much
I lacked.
      Gestur the poet's son killed by
      lightning

We see in each fact, not the fable
As feebly we search and appraise,
That law, if illucid, is stable
And leaves but one prospect to face;
To think not in hours, but in ages,
At eve not to claim all our wages
Will bring out the best in the race.
   — **Brothers' Destiny**

No horns were blown nor havoc
made
When He was in the Manger laid.
No diary the date has shown;
His date of birth is still unknown.
His catechism was common toil,
His copy-book the living soil.
Where nature, old, yet all abloom,
In every knoll concealed a tomb.
   — Eloi Lamma Sabahkthani

Wisdom, goodwill, goodness,
perfection
are in no way innate to humanity
from
creation; they only come from the
heavy, lashing experiences of
succeeding generations.
      Letters and Essays

1. Loftur Bjarnason, **Anthology of Icelandic Literature**, Berkley California, University Extension Service, University of California, Vol. II, 1961 pp. 215 - 216.

2. **Icelandic Canadian Magazine**, Summer 1973 pp. 15 - 17.

3. Stephan G. Stephansson, **Bréf og Rit**, Vol. I, page 10.

4. Ibid. Vol. I, page 10.

5. Ibid. Vol. IV, page 153.

6,7,8. Extracts from **Sameining**, published by the Icelandic Lutheran Synod in Winnipeg.

9. This may have appeared in **Heimskringla**, the Winnipeg Icelandic weekly which espoused Unitarianism. (It's rival, **Lögberg**, favored Lutheranism.)

10. From **Sameining**.

11. Kirconnell, Canadian linguist, translated the poetry of Stephansson and others into English.

12,13,14. Nordal, Kristjánsson, and Halldórsson are Icelandic scholars of recent times.

15,16,17. Stephan G. Stephanson, **Bréf og Rit**, Vol. I, page 10. The following names of periodicals and books indicate some of the reading done by Stephansson: **The New Ideal** (Boston); **Boston Investigator**; **Iron Clad Age** (Indianapolis); **Truth Seeker** (New York); **Free Thought** (San Francisco); **Secular Thought** (Toronto); **The Industrialist** (Denver); **Freethinker's Magazine** (Buffalo). He also recommends B.F. Underwood's **Debates and Essays**. A well read copy is in his personal library.

18. Stow Persons, **Free Religion: An American Faith** (New Haven, 1947) page 131.

19. Partial paraphrase and quotation from Francis Ellington Abbot in Stow Persons, op. cit. p. 66.

20. Ibid. p. 54.

21. Ibid. p. 91.

22. Loftur Bjarnason, op. cit. pp. 215 - 216.

23. **Lögberg** Feb., 1927.

GEB and CCW

Chapter 5

The First Unitarian Missionary to The Icelandic Settlements Björn Pétursson

The Icelandic Cultural Society, as has been noted, was organized in 1888. It was modelled, according to its guiding spirit Stephan G. Stephansson, after the Ethical Culture Societies of the time, and more than likely the Liberal Leagues and other such groups which were to be found in many cities at the time. Rare, however, it must have been, that such a group should be organized by and for a group of immigrant farmers in remote Dakota Territory. One of the early members was Stephansson's neighbor and friend, Björn Pétursson, (1826-1893) who by that time was a "Unitarian missionary". The story of Pétursson is the story of the organized beginnings of a Unitarian movement among the Icelandic settlers, but the evidence points to Stephansson, the free thinker, as the source of the information and ideas and contacts which were so important to Pétursson.

Many years later Stephansson, in a letter to a friend, reminisced about his friend Björn Pétursson, who was 27 years his senior:

> I knew him here in the west. He kept up with the
> thought of the day more than those who were

younger and considered themselves better educated; but he did not really blossom because of his great conciliatory nature of toleration, even when his own burning interests were at stake. He took the unmerciful answers and attacks of his opponents with grace. And I know of only one of them of whom he said any angry words.

He told me a story from Parliament to this effect: 'When I entered, there were only two parties, learned men and farmers. Both claimed me. The learned men because I attended the Bessastaðir School, and the farmers because I farmed. I could not follow either party, and was frustrated and powerless. I could not follow the learned party because they considered nothing more than their own welfare. With the farmers I was out of tune. They were too stupid, and didn't see how the others used them.'

Björn was sometimes my guest in Dakota. Many things were discussed. One time he brought up the idea of individual immortality. We argued it back and forth. I was tired, wanting to sleep because it was nearing daylight. Björn had often repeated his arguments because all the new reasons had been used up. 'Now I do not want to argue with you anymore, Björn,' I said crossly. 'We have done nothing for some time but rehash the same points'.

Björn did not answer, but rolled over in bed laughing. I asked him what was tickling him.

'Now I have found out what I wanted, and I shall quit.' said Björn. 'I thought it was impossible to argue with you to the point that you got angry, but at last I succeeded. Now I know you can become angry.'

Of course I wasn't angry, but I let Björn believe it

without questioning him, when I saw that he had
been using me. [1]

We can be quite certain that in the course of this
acquaintanceship, Stephansson shared not only his ideas with
Pétursson, but also whatever printed matter he had, whether
books, periodicals or tracts, for both of them read and spoke
English. More than likely this included the **Index** and the
Debates and Essays of Underwood. It is fairly accurate
speculation that through their reading they learned about
Unitarianism, and after the **Index** ceased publication in 1886,
the remaining subscribers were transferred to **Unity,** an
avowedly Unitarian periodical edited in Chicago by Jenkin
Lloyd Jones. Ads were placed regularly in **Unity** by the Post
Office Mission offering tracts, pamphlets, and other literature,
and it was the Post Office Mission to which Pétursson wrote in
1886.

The Post Office Mission was an effort to reach potential
Unitarians by circulating tracts and publications of the
American Unitarian Association, as well as, in some cases,
sermons. "A frail, little woman, hopelessly deaf and suffering
from an incurable disease",[2] named Miss Sallie Ellis, wanted to
do something for Unitarianism before she died, and in 1881
with the help of her minister, Charles W. Wendte, and the
Women's Auxiliary of Cincinnati, she systematized the project
by first placing ads in daily papers. The response was
unexpected and the project was taken up by other Women's
groups in Unitarian churches as well as by the Western
Unitarian Conference office in Chicago:

> Only four and one-half years were permitted to Miss
> Ellis in which to accomplish her work. ... During
> this period she wrote 2,500 letters, sent out 22,000
> tracts and papers, sold 286 books, and loaned 258.
> ... Through her influence, several young men
> entered the ministry who are today doing effective
> work. She saved several persons from doubt and
> despair, gave strength to the weak and comfort to
> those that mourned. At her death in 1885, the letters
> received from many of her correspondents showed
> how strong and deep had been her influence.[3]

William Channing Gannett, at that time minister of Unity Unitarian Church in St. Paul, is credited with "christening" this work *The Post Office Mission.* During Gannett's ministry in St. Paul, a Post Office Mission secretary was named, who was responsible for correspondence in the Upper Midwest, or as it was more often called the Northwest.

In 1886, Björn Pétursson made an inquiry to the Unitarian Post Office Mission and here begins the story of the Icelandic Unitarian Mission. His inquiry was answered by Miss Jennie Elizabeth McCaine of St. Paul, and she further wrote the Reverend Grindall Reynolds, Secretary of the American Unitarian Association in Boston:

St. Paul, Dec. 2, 1886

Rev. Grindall Reynolds:
Dear Sir:

Through my Post Office Mission work, I have discovered an individual who seems anxious in some way to carry the good news of our liberal faith to the unsatisfied minds among his countrymen, the Icelanders. I am not able to tell him much about our missionary fund and shall refer him to you for futher information.

I copy paragraphs from some of his recent letters that you may get some idea of the man and what he would like to do. If such translations as he speaks of would be made I think they would be very useful. There are many Icelanders already in the North West and more coming each year. Occasionally I receive applications from them for our literature but they all tell me that few of their people read English.

This man seems trustworthy so far as I can judge from his letters and might perhaps become a co-worker in the missionary field, could financial assistance be given him. Should you think it best I hope you will communicate with him; his address is Bjorn Peterson,* Hallson, Dakota. The following are extracts from his letters:

*Björn Pétursson used the anglicized spelling, **Peterson,** in his correspondence with people who used English.

Oct. 15th — I am fully satisfied that I belong to your church, heart and soul. I was educated for the ministry in my own country (Iceland) but when I got through college I could not prevail on my conscience to preach dogmas I did not believe in myself so I gave it up. I recognize in the Unitarian movement the reformation I have long hoped for and expected and should be glad to get a chance to promote the same among my countrymen which on the whole are very intelligent people and not so priest-ridden and orthodox as their relatives, the Norwegians. Have the Unitarians any fund for missionary purposes? What is the strength of your church in the United States and other countries?

Nov. 26th — I have friends and relatives in every Icelandic settlement both in this country and Canada. In addition, I beg to say that I am favorably known among my countrymen having in the old country held offices of public trust, and among them the membership of the legislative assembly for three successive terms (9 years). In 1876 I emigrated to Canada and in three years I lost my whole property in the swamps of the Icelandic reserve on the west shore of Lake Winnipeg....

What I could do to promote our cause among my country people in the most practicable way is a question not easy but very difficult to solve. The Icelandic tongue is the old Scandinavian language from which the modern Scandinavian languages are derived, probably as old as Greek and Latin, and with a grammar as difficult. Some few Icelanders can read English books, and some more Norwegian-Danish but most of them can't read either. Therefore, I think it most practicable to translate some of your best tracts for distribution through the post-offices in the Icelandic settlements. In Winnipeg there is a good paper recently started which I think will have a wide circulation on this

side of the Atlantic and in the old country, by name
Heimskringla (Cosmos). To publish Unitarian
articles or something in the line of free thought in
religious matters, would, I think, be to the point,
and do much good. I could, and am very willing to
do this provided I could get sufficient pecuniary
assistance. I know many free-thinkers among my
countrymen and am sure there are many more of
them than anyone has any idea about. I fear, too,
there are some atheists, though I know only one, the
chief editor of **Heimskringla** who is a scholar from
the University of Copenhagen and a relation of
mine.

Hoping that you will consider this "discovery" and
let me hear from you in regard to it. I remain yours
most respectfully.

Miss J.E. McCaine,
194 Pleasant Ave.,
P.O.M. agent for Minn. 4

Björn Pétursson was born in the east of Iceland on August
22, 1826, the son of a minister who served a very sparsely
populated area. As a young man he attended schools in the
Reykjavik area, including the famed Bessastaðir Academy and
chose a course of study that seemed to head in the direction of
preparing for the ministry. He had but one year left when the
students rebelled against their rector who was temporarily
suspended for questioning. The rector was subsequently
reinstated, but many of the students, including Pétursson did
not return; also, he apparently had doubts about the ministry
and many of the church's teachings. Thus in 1846 he returned
to eastern Iceland and took up farming. On October 2, 1850, he
married a minister's daughter from the area, Ólafía Ólafsdóttir,
sister of the poet Páll Ólafsson* and half-sister of Jón Olafsson,
editor of **Heimskringla**. His farming does not appear to have
been successful for he moved from farm to farm for the next
twenty years.

*Páll Ólafsson was a 19th century Icelandic lyric poet.

But during this period he also served as a member of the Parliament or Althing for three sessions (1861-1869), and as an alternate for a member who could not attend for one session (1873). This period in the history of Iceland saw the rise of many restless and freedom-aspiring people who were hoping for the independence 5 of the island nation, inspired and led by the great nationalist Jón Sigurðsson. Apparently, however, Pétursson's lack of oratorical skills and his temperament precluded his distinction in the Althing, although he was held in respect by all with whom he worked. One of his biographers, Thorleifur Jackson, wrote of him many years later:

> Björn was an intelligent man, tall and dignified in stature, strong and agile. He had to the end good use of what he had learned in school, for instance, Latin. He had skill in teaching young people. He was entertaining and cheerful, especially in the company of friends and everything that was depressing had to yield to cheer. He was friendly, and had a great interest in his country's welfare. 6

The famous volcano, Hekla, erupted in 1875 spewing ash throughout the eastern part of Iceland. Very hard times ensued, driving many people from their farms, among them Björn Pétursson. Like many others, he set sail for America with many of his countrymen to seek a less harsh and difficult life. He first settled in New Iceland at a place called Sandy Bar on the west shore of Lake Winnipeg, near the present community of Riverton. High water and pestilence caused many of these new settlers, including the Pétursson family to move again, this time in 1878 to Pembina County in Dakota Territory. There was apparently a restlessness in Pétursson for he spent the year 1880-81 in Iceland. Tragic news reached him in Iceland as he was about to depart for home, informing him that his son, Páll Björnsson, a promising physician, had died suddenly at his home in Houston, Minnesota.* This was a great blow. He then returned to North Dakota, where, in 1884, his wife Ólafía died. After her death, it seems that he divided his time among his children, who at that time all lived in Pembina County.

In this period Pétursson appears to have begun serious

---

*This version seems correct, but cf. variation in Appendix H.

thinking about religion, which led to his communication with Miss McCaine. She wrote to Mr. Reynolds who, in turn, made contact with Kristofer Janson who then headed a Norwegian Unitarian mission in Minneapolis and Brown County, Minnesota. Janson was receiving a subsidy or grant from the A.U.A. Miss McCaine followed through on her "discovery" for the Unitarian mission field as indicated in this letter of Feb. 11, 1887:

> I received in due time your reply to my letter and forwarded the same to Mr. Peterson together with Mr. Janson's address. I learn that they have exchanged letters and that Mr. Peterson has empowered Mr. Janson to arrange the matter with you in his behalf if possible. I hope you will be be able to make some arrangement by which Mr. P. can be helped to do the work he offers to do. I am convinced that he is a trustworthy man and that such translations would be very helpful in our missionary work. It is not often that we find a man with ability to do this work who is willing to give his time and labor, and when found, should be utilized. [7]

Kristofer Janson, as Miss McCaine indicates, wasted little time contacting Mr. Pétursson and offered to grant him some money from his funds to help translate and publish some pamphlets. In Janson's report of late February 1887 he writes:

> I have taken temporary care of the Icelander, Bjorn Peterson, who corresponded with the secretary, Rev. Grindall Reynolds, asking for help to publish some Unitarian pamphlets in the Icelandic language. According to my plan he has now translated two of my pamphlets, and when they are printed in Winnipeg, he will follow, himself, and deliver some lectures about Unitarian principles and then have those printed pamphlets for sale wherever he speaks.... I have paid Mr. Peterson $20 for his translations and will pay the cost of the printing

from my book fund. I have also promised him $25
to start the lecture trip. 8

A little more than a month later, Mr. Janson writes Mr.
Reynolds:

> My Icelander, Mr. Peterson, is now in Winnipeg,
> preparing his campaign. Two of my sermons are
> translated and paid for, and he will now commence
> lecturing. 9

In early June of that same year, Mr. Janson reports that
"Peterson" has translated a third pamphlet.

Petursson was free to travel so long as he had the financial
means since he was retiring from farming. His first "door-to-
door" missionary endeavor was in Pembina and Cavalier
Counties in North Dakota:

> ...mostly walking from house to house, and
> lecturing where I can gather any number together.
> On the whole I have met with a better reception
> than I expected. ... Owing to the activity of the
> orthodox on one side and the inactivity of the
> liberals on the other, we must, in order to secure a
> good harvest, do something more than scatter the
> seed. The Icelanders, generally, are a quiet,
> thinking, intelligent people, open for a sound
> argumentation and reason. Therfore [sic], in my
> opinion, there is nothing so effective, so exactly to
> the point, as a travelling missioner who could visit
> all the Icelandic settlements in Canada and the U.S.
> in order to lecture on the various orthodox
> absurdities and discuss the whole subject. I myself is
> [sic] not only willing but glad to undertake such a
> mission, principally among my own people, and
> occasionally among the other Scandinavian
> nationalities, provided that I could get the necessary
> financial assistance from the missionary funds of the
> A.U.A., as I have no means of my own. Of course, I
> think $500 a year would not prove too much, if the

missioner is to be enabled to subsist and travel between and through the many far distant settlements as a gentleman. If you either think this too much or the mission fund can't afford it, I shall gladly accept a lesser sum and work for it conscientiously, so far it goes [sic]. As to my own self I can't tell you anything except what I have already told my friends, Mr. Janson and Miss McCaine, and as they, through our frequent correspondence, must have formed some definite idea, and, so far as I know, a true one about my character and ability, I will ask them to give their opinion. 10

This is Pétursson's first request directly for an A.U.A. grant, and as was to be a frequent occurrence, the A.U.A. committee and Mr. Reynolds were slow in responding to the request. Up to this point Mr. Janson had provided him with modest sums mainly for publication of the tracts. Mr. Janson twice during the summer had urged favorable action on the request, but not until September 13, did he receive a reply — with a cheque. Pétursson wasted no time to prepare a trip to Winnipeg:

Early in Oct. I started for Canada and stayed there about 2 months, working every day more or less according to opportunities for my problem: To liberalize the religious opinions of my country people. In Winnipeg there are about 1,000 Icelanders ... not belonging to the Lutheran or any other congregation, scattered all over the vast city. In order to reach them I had to content myself with small audiences in private houses here and there. Although I met with much indifference in religious matters, and even in some few instances, atheism, I was much pleased to perceive a marked advance in our liberal Christian opinions, as a result of Mr. Janson's pamphlets, translated and distributed by myself in Winnipeg last winter.
Altogether I have travelled about 500 miles forward and back.

The topics lectured on and discussed are (the) following:

1 The theological doctrine of the Trinity, its origin and lack of any Scriptural foundations.

2 What Christ did say about himself and the teaching of the apostles, Paul and Peter concerning his personality.

3 Objections to the orthodox dogma of eternal punishment. Prayer having no effect on God, but benefitting and elevating oneself.

4 Orthodoxy itself the principal cause of the unbelief, indifference and atheism among the Christian peoples.

5 The noble work and aim of the liberal Christians, especially the Unitarians.

6 The trials (and) disasters afflicting humanity not such directly by God as punishment but a natural consequence of the human transgressions, ignorance (and) folly according to the divine law and order.

Besides this I have occasionally treated various other topics.

Over 3 weeks ago I got chilled on my way homewards. (I) have been very low from inflammation of the lungs, and am still very weak and unable to work. Whenever I feel well I intend to continue my missionary work in my own locality so far (as I am) able in the severity of the North Dakota winters.

By returning mail, please send me my quart. annual allowance as I have promised to pay my contracted debts at the middle of next month. Accept my best wishes for your happiness in the New Year, beginning tomorrow. [11]

During the winter of 1888 he remained at home in North Dakota and "could do nothing except to keep up a constant correspondence." [12] In this same letter he reports on the organization of the Icelandic Cultural Society in which Stephan G. Stephansson was an instrumental force, "for the purpose of investigating into religious matters and seeking general enlightenment and progress in all what constitutes a true manliness. This society will, I am sure, be a great help to our cause in the future."

After the middle of March he is back on the circuit:

> On the 22nd March I started out on the prairies in the vicinity of my country home in Cavalier Co. and am just come home. I have travelled mostly on foot, from house to house, often wading through a knee deep packed snow. In this way I have visited some 19 family houses, held my lectures and afterwards discussed the topics lectured on, with some members of the families, who all in all number about 100 persons. Besides the topics mentioned in my last report, I have held an exhaustive lecture on the Lutheran doctrine of justification by mere faith in the atonement (and the) vicarious sacrifice of Jesus Christ, proving that it were not only an absurdity, a blasphemy, but also, wholly, contradictory to the teachings of Christ himself. In some few cases I met with a decided opposition from the old folks but on the whole, the resistance is gradually giving way, and some of the younger and most intelligent are coming over on our side. My effort has been to set people athinking and investigation for themselves. [13]

This promotion of the Unitarian faith by Pétursson continued in his "home county" during the spring of 1888, and in addition to home visits he gave three public lectures.

Pétursson had been a Unitarian missionary for almost a year and a half, and his efforts would have been impossible without the support and promotion of Jennie McCaine and Kristofer Janson. But he had met neither of them and knew them only through correspondence. So when he made a trip to the Twin Cities and on to the Icelandic settlements in southwestern Minnesota, he visited both sponsors. Miss McCaine's faith in him and his work increased:

Having become personally acquainted with Mr. Peterson I find him all we trusted him to be. A man of great intelligence, thoroughly interested in his work, and in every way well fitted for it. Having the the full confidence and respect of his people he cannot fail to do a good work among them. 14

Janson on the other hand had some reservations:

Our Icelandic worker Mr. Peterson paid me a visit in the spring ...... Let him continue his lecturing and preaching and fighting, and I hope he will pick up some young Icelander to send to Meadville who will be able when through to start a congregation up there in Manitoba. Mr. Peterson himself is too old to take on his shoulders such a burden. 15

This trip to Lyon and Lincoln countries in southwestern Minnesota was the first of two trips Pétursson was to make as a Unitarian missionary.. He went there with the conviction that many people in those Icelandic communities were dissatisfied with the Lutheranism being preached to them. He describes their pastor thus:

although a young man and a graduate from the University of Christiana Norway (he) is a religious crank. His fanatical worship of Christ is, by and by becoming too much even for the orthodox members of his congregation. 16

After a month visiting and preaching around the area, he returned to Pembina County convinced that religious liberalism was both needed and desired in these settlements.

Less than a year later, March 1889, Pétursson returned to the Minnesota settlement, and in a letter to Grindall Reynolds his motives become clear:

Although the minister be a young man and lastly educated at Christiana, Norway, he is an ultra orthodox, a sort of religious crank, preaching Christ almost alone as God and Savior. Owing partly to this and partly to the spreading of our liberal ideas there is a growing discontent with the minister even among his personal friends and adherents which sooner or later must come to a crisis. If he could be removed from thence, there is a good place for Rev. M. Jockumson as most of the population want him. At my instigation some of my liberal friends are now working for that purpose, and very much I desire their success because I think Mr. Jockumson shall prove a valuable acquisition to our field. [17]

Meanwhile the minister and the faithful in the congregation at Minneota, the center of this settlement, were well aware of the agitation seemingly caused by Mr. Pétursson On Sunday, March 31, 1889, the minister called a congregational meeting to discuss the reaction of the membership to Mr. Pétursson's work in their area. They then voted unanimously:

This congregation believes that it is its Christian duty to shun completely Björn Pétursson as a missionary. [18]

The references, both years, in Mr. Pétursson's reports on his trips to Minneota to the Rev. Matthías Jochumsson of Iceland are worth noting. It appears that one of his hopes or dreams from the beginning was to bring Jochumsson to America. He shared this dream with Janson in 1887:

His hope is to stir up his countrymen for liberal views to such an extent that they be willing to form a liberal society, and then induce Matthías Jokumsen one of the most prominent and accepted Icelandic preachers and poets to come as minister. This Mr. Jokumsen is a thoroughly liberal man and perfectly versed in the English language. He has among other things translated **Macbeth** into Icelandic. Could you get him, you had won the battle, I suppose. [19]

The next major references in the extant correspondence of
Pétursson is in relation to Minneota and the Icelandic
settlement of Lyon and Lincoln counties. But as time passed,
these hopes became dimmer for Pétursson as he records his
sentiments in a letter in Sept. 1888 to Grindall Reynolds:

> As the Icel. population in Winnipeg is, by far, the
> largest at one place in Canada, I decided to give it
> my whole time and work this season. My principal
> aim was to prepare there a place for Rev. M.
> Jockumson who as you probably know is a
> Unitarian, though, for many years by force of
> circumstances, (is) a minister in the Luth. State
> Church of Iceland. As Rev. Jockumson for many
> reasons has been a general favorite of his country
> people, I had the best hopes of success in this
> undertaking. But on being told by immigrants to W.
> from the old country, even by Mr. Jockumson's
> own parishioners, that he was no longer his former
> self, but a weak, disheartened and extremely poor
> man with a big family (9 children), I concluded that
> I must give up my favorite idea although it grieved
> me very much. He is, anyhow, no match for the
> young, active and energetic Luth. ministers here and
> their fanatical adherents. [20]

In light of this letter it is a little puzzling that some seven
months later when he was in Minneota, he again expresses the
idea of bringing Jochumsson to serve a parish in America. But
essentially this is the last reference to be found in Pétursson's
letters to the possibility of Jochumsson accepting a call to a
Canadian or American congregation. In passing, it can be
noted that Jochumsson did come to Winnipeg and North
Dakota somewhat later, in 1893, enroute to the Chicago
Exposition, and in his memoirs he is less than complimentary
about Björn Pétursson and the Unitarian congregation.

Shortly after Pétursson returned home to North Dakota
from his first Minneota trip he was by reports keeping a busy
speaking schedule. He spoke to the Icelandic Cultural Society
on June 10 (1888) on Unitarianism: "What Unitarians do

believe and what not, their noble work as defenders and propagators of the true, genuine Christianity etc. etc." On June 23rd he spoke about the establishment of a new monthly paper in Icelandic:

> for the purpose of propagating liberal ideas and defending our cause, and ourselves against the malicious attacks and insinuations of the orthodox fanatics who have secured for themselves both of the Icelandic weeklies issued in Winnipeg, and besides have a monthly of their own edited by their foreman and leader, Rev. J. Bjarnason, Winnipeg. .... Could you advise or do something for us in this matter? 21

The most interesting June meeting was in connection with the Annual Conference of the Icelandic Lutheran Synod held at Mountain, North Dakota. Pétursson reports on this debate:

> The 25th inst. I and my people in this locality had a debate on the question: 'Does the Luth. church permit and favor free investigation?' ... invited to do so by the orthodox party. There were attending all the Luth. Ministers (4), 30 delegates from the different congregations in Canada and North Dakota and besides a number of other leading orthodox people in the vicinity of Mountain. Altogether there were present ca. 300. I made the most possible out of the occasion assisted by 4 able speakers of my men, the Liberals. The debate turned out a success for the Liberals so much that even many of the orthodox themselves were fair enough to admit it. 22

This meeting was very fully reported in the then new Icelandic weekly, **Lögberg** and the text of the debate is reported in full. The meeting opened with a short address by the Rev. Jón Bjarnason in which he maintained that Lutheran (as well as all Protestant) churches support unfettered research. The distinctiveness of the Protestant world is that it supports research and is, indeed, itself born of such openness as characterizes research. He went on to add that no one should be misled because the church does have some propositions that are unchanging and absolute, and yet no one is prohibited from examining anything because the church is certain of its verities.

Björn Pétursson spoke at least twice and asserted that although he was glad to hear that the church supports research, his experience proved otherwise and noted especially the plight of Magnús Eiríksson. 23

Skapti Brynjólfsson, a N.D. State Senator and a member of the Cultural Society, brought up evolution and evolutionary theory, and expressed confusion about what the Lutheran clergy meant by unfettered research. Another person suggested that the clergy would do well to spend some time researching the contradictions of the Old Testament rather than propounding their doctrines.

The debate continued for three hours!

On this note of success in the Debates, Björn Pétursson left for Winnipeg and a summer of missionary work there. It was less successful than his visit the previous summer:

In Winnipeg I held 2 public lectures in July, the 1st on the question: Is the Luteran doctrine of justification by faith alone consistent with the teachings of Christ? The 2nd: Is the doctrine of Trinity, the godhead of Jesu Christ, and the Holy Ghost taught by Christ himself and his apostles?

Through the leading Icel. newspaper (Lögberg) in Winnipeg, I invited all the orthodox Luterans to attend and defend the chief doctrines of their church, but they were wise enough not to risk it. The trustees tried, in vain, to prevail on their Minister, Rev. J. Bjarnason, the head man of the Icel. Luterans on this continent.

Under the circumstances the Orthodox fanatics could not do anything else than by all means to prevent attendance from others. In this they succeeded so far that I had only small audiences." 24

He seemed to have been more successful in holding meetings in private homes and in visiting people and discussing Unitarianism with them. At the end of August he again returned home to Pembina County.

Perhaps the greatest highlight for Pétursson during the year 1888 was attendance at the Second Annual meeting of the Minnesota Unitarian Conference in St. Cloud. Here he had the opportunity to meet the Rev. Grindall Reynolds, Secretary of the A.U.A., with whom he had regularly corresponded; also leaders of the Western Unitarian Conference as well as the Unitarian ministers in Minnesota.

The minutes record:

> Mr. Bjorne [sic] Petursson of Alma D.T. was in attendance as a guest of the conference. Bjorne Petursson read an account of his work during the year among the 10,000 Icelanders now residing in the Northwest, for the most part house to house visits, explaining the principles of Unitarianism and disseminating our literature.

Pétursson reveals his enthusiasm for the St. Cloud meeting in a letter to Mr. Reynolds:

> I was so favorably impressed with all what I saw and heard at St. Cloud, that I desire to be formally accepted as a member of the (Western Conference) and admitted to the Unitarian ministry if you consider me qualified to. ... I think it might, occasionally, do some good if I be ordained as a travelling minister. 25

Here for the first time, but certainly not the last because he persists until his death in 1893, Björn Pétursson brings up the question of Unitarian ordination. The very question brings up some doubts in the mind of Grindall Reynolds. Reynolds appears to have some reservations about the whole Icelandic mission from the very beginning, but always somewhat reluctantly supports it. Kristofer Janson, after meeting Pétursson in the spring of 1888 has qualified enthusiasm for Pétursson but not the project, as he reveals in a letter in 1889:

> If Mr. Peterson had been the right man, young, vigorous, eloquent, I would say: 'by all means

enable him to settle down in Winnipeg.' ... I sent an inquiring letter about him to Winnipeg the time he asked for ordination. The informations received were such, that I opposed his being ordained as our representative. Not that they said anything unfavorable about his character, but they said that he was too old and not the man to take it up with his younger and more vigorous opponents of the Lutheran faith, that he had not the power to fascinate his countrymen, that his delivery was tedious, etc. [26]

Another indication of the ambivalence with which the A.U.A. viewed the Icelandic project, was the funding process .. if it could be called a process. The A.U.A. Board almost every year was late in acting upon the request for funds, and making clear the stipulations they had in mind. And even when the grants had been approved, usually $500 per annum, the quarterly payments were tardy. Fortunately for Pétursson he had a most effective advocate in Miss Jennie McCaine.

Pétursson refers in his correspondence occasionally to the opposition of the "Luteran fanatics" and identifies the leader as the Rev. Jón Bjarnason, then Synod president. Bjarnason was a close relative of his family and seems to have been his personal good friend. Bjarnason was not silent, but instead of attacking Pétursson or directly challenging him, directed his attacks against Kristofer Janson.

1. Translated by the author from a letter written by Stephansson.
2. G.W. Cooke, **Unitarianism in America** (Boston, 1902), P.289.
3. Ibid., 290.
4. J.E. McCaine to Grindall Reynolds, Dec. 2,1886.
5. Iceland was at the time politically and economically subservient to Denmark.
6. Translated by the author from a biographic sketch written in Icelandic by Thorleifur Jackson.
7. McCaine to Reynolds, Feb.11, 1887. A.U.A. letterbooks.
8. Kristofer Janson, Quarterly Report, Feb. 24, 1887. A.U.A. letterbooks.
9. Janson to Reynolds, April 2, 1887. A.U.A. letterbooks.
10. Bjorn Peterson to Reynolds, June 14,1887. A.U.A. letterbooks.
11. Peterson to Reynolds, Dec. 31, 1887. A.U.A. letterbooks.
12. Peterson to Reynolds, March 31, 1888. A.U.A. letterbooks.

13. Ibid.

14. McCaine to Reynolds, June 24, 1888. A.U.A. letterbooks.

15. Janson, Quarterly Report, Aug. 24, 1888. A.U.A. letterbooks.

16. Peterson to Reynolds, June 30, 1888. A.U.A. letterbooks.

17. Peterson to Reynolds, March 31, 1889. A.U.A. letterbooks.

18. From the minutes of a Lutheran Congregational Meeting in Mineota, MN.

19. Janson to Reynolds, June 8, 1887. A.U.A. letterbooks.

20. Peterson to Reynolds, Sept. 30, 1888. A.U.A. letterbooks.

21. Peterson to Reynolds, June 30, 1888. A.U.A. letterbooks.

22. Ibid.

23. Magnús Eiríksson (See Chapter 2) graduated from a Lutheran Theological College in Denmark, but was later ostracized for his non-conformist views.

24. Peterson to Reynolds, Sept. 30, 1888. A.U.A. letterbooks.

25. Peterson to Reynolds, Dec. 31, 1888. A.U.A. letterbooks.

26. Janson to Reynolds, Oct. 25,1889. A.U.A. letterbooks.

Chapter 6

Religion and Romance
Jennie Elizabeth
McCaine Peterson

Accounts of the beginnings of Unitarianism among Icelanders in America have generally credited Kristofer Janson with being the main contact with Björn Pétursson. The research of this author indicates that actually this is a misstatement, and that the pivotal person was Jennie Elizabeth McCaine of St. Paul. We have already noted in Chapter 5 that the initial Unitarian contact Pétursson had was with McCaine and that it was she who put him into contact with both Grindall Reynolds of the A.U.A. and Mr. Janson.

Jennie Elizabeth McCaine was born in Francestown, New Hampshire, on March 16, 1838. She was the youngest of a large family, and was 2 years old when her mother died. She was raised by an aunt in Henniker, NH, and later returned to live with her father until she moved to St. Paul in 1859. Dr. Rögnvaldur Pétursson says of her in her obituary of 1918:

> Her father, David McCaine, was of Scottish descent, remarkably liberal and catholic in his religious beliefs ... and his daughter inherited her ideas quite naturally from him. He was opposed to slavery and was more active than most

contemporaries in the Anti-slavery movement. Thus early in life she accepted the centrality of fairness and humaneness, and she dedicated her life to those principles.. She was committed to all she undertook and was faithful to all whom she considered friends. [1]

She moved to St. Paul in 1859 with her sister, Mrs. William H. Grant, and her family when St. Paul was a small but important community on the banks of the Mississippi. Her brother, David McCaine, was also a St. Paul pioneer and an attorney, and both he and their brother-in-law William H. Grant are listed as members of a Minnesota Regiment in the Civil War. Not much information can be found about Miss McCaine during her early St. Paul years (the St. Paul City Register did not list unmarried women during that period).

She was a charter member of Unity Church when it was organized in 1872 and one can assume that she was part of the group that attempted to start a Unitarian congregation even earlier. Her brother was one of the original trustees of the new church and served in that capacity for a number of years. Samuel M. Crothers, her minister in St. Paul in the late 80's, reported that she worked in publicity and promotion for her church. The church published a 4-page information pamphlet in 1874 and here Jennie McCaine is listed as Amusements Chairman. That year she played "Chatter", the maid, in a farce called "The Deadshot". She was listed as an officer of "The True Helpers", a temperance society in the church. But of most interest to us is that in 1887, she is listed as an officer in the "Pamphlet Mission", which one can presume to be the predecessor to the "Post Office Mission". For a decade she worked, as Crothers put it, in "publicity and promotion for her church" before she was elected General Secretary of the Post Office Mission of the Minnesota Unitarian Conference at its organizational meeting in 1887.

It was thus no accident that she received Björn Pétursson's inquiries about Unitarianism in October and November 1886. She reports that she "occasionally (receives) applications from them (Icelanders) for our literature." From her St. Paul vantage point she had undoubtedly gained a very positive attitude towards Scandinavians who were then emigrating in great numbers into Minnesota and not the least into Minneapolis. She wrote:

> The Scandinavian element in this country promises a good harvest to liberal thought in the years to come ... and no one can reach them so readily as one of their own people. If the Icelanders continue to emigrate as fast as they have for a few years past, we shall soon have the entire population of the island here. And a more intelligent class of people it would be hard to find. [2]

A few years later, reflecting upon her lot, she says, "Some unseen power seems to have led me from one place to another, wherever my services were most needed." [3] This serves as good an explanation as any perhaps of the great interest she was to take in Björn Pétursson and the Icelandic Mission. At first she assisted Pétursson in organizing this mission; in due course she became an integral part of it.

The closing of her initial letter to Grindall Reynolds in 1886 has a charm to it even as it is direct: "Hoping that you will consider this 'discovery' and let me hear from you in regard to it." [4] Björn Pétursson and the Icelanders were a "discovery" for her and for her Unitarianism. This Post Office Mission contact was not taken casually by her either; for about 2 months later she follows up with another letter to Grindall Reynolds.

There is another role or perhaps another facet of her role to make certain that her "discovery" is not forgotten that she undertakes frequently. This is to jog the A.U.A. and Mr. Reynolds to continue to grant Pétursson a stipend, and then to send him his cheques regularly. Her letters in this matter are at first gentle but firm:

> One year ago I wrote asking the A.U.A. give Mr. Peterson five hundred dollars for missionary work among his people, the Icelanders, in this country. In doing this I felt that I was asking you to take Mr. Peterson upon trust, and felt very grateful for the confidence shown in me and in my judgment when

the appropriation was made. I am happy to say that this year I am able to speak from personal knowledge of the man. Having become personally acquainted with Mr. Peterson I find him all that we trusted him to be. A man of great intelligence, thoroughly interested in his work, and in every way well fitted for it. Having the full confidence and respect of his people he cannot fail to do a good work among them.

The five hundred dollars scarcely more than pays for traveling expenses so large is the field of his labor, but as he has many friends in nearly every settlement who are willing to entertain him, he is able to get along with that, and is altogether too modest to ask for more.. I hope however, that you will consider this matter another year and if possible give him six hundred. [5]

Unfortunately, this was not to be last but only the first of Miss McCaine's letters on the matter of money. When in late September of 1888, 3 months after the above letter, nothing had been heard, Mr. Reynolds received another one:

I learn through the report in the last **Register** that at the September meeting of the board no appropriation was made for the continuance of Mr. Peterson's work: from this I infer that either the appropriation was refused or that no action was taken at that meeting upon his case. I hope the latter, for it would seem exceedingly foolish to drop a work so well begun, and which so far as I can learn has been satisfactory and promises good returns in the future. It were better never begun, if it is to be dropped now. Please let me know whether action was taken or postponed as I am arranging for him to be present at State Conference next month where I had hoped he would have the pleasure of meeting you. If his work is to be discontinued I do not think he would care to come nor would it be worth while to have him. Hoping to hear from you at once. [6]

In two weeks Mr. Pétursson had a cheque!

This was a role which was to continue for Jennie McCaine, that of being an adversary of the A.U.A. whenever it seemed to falter in its support of the Icelandic Mission. In one respect Miss McCaine could be said to have the "conscience in Boston". T.B. Forbush, later to be much on the scene with the Winnipeg mission, stated the relationship between her and the A.U.A. very bluntly:

> Did you know Mr. Peterson and Miss McCaine were married? The husband of your fiercest foe in St. Paul is now on your salary list!

Miss McCaine had other roles in respect to the Icelandic Mission and Björn Pétursson One of these was as a "mentor" perhaps, or at least teacher of liberal religious thought, especially in the Western Conference. There is no doubt that her own theological leanings were more to the Western Conference and its more liberal stance, than towards the Christian stance of the A.U.A. This should surprise no one, for she had been a parishioner of William Channing Gannett for the 7 years he was minister in St. Paul. His was an inclusivist view of liberal religion, characterized in capsule:

> Is Western Unitarianism ready to give up its Christian character? No. Is it ready to exclude from its full fellowship those who do not take the name of Christian or Theist? No.

Jennie M. Peterson preached quite often for her husband during their ministry in Winnipeg, for ill health plagued him frequently, and after his death she served as minister of the church and preached about half the time. Only one of her sermons is extant, and it has been translated into Icelandic. If it is typical, it reflects the philosophy of evolutionary religion rather common in Western Conference churches, witnessing frequently to the findings of the sciences of the day. It does not do justice to her sermon to excerpt a few sentences from it, but this will give us the flavor of her religious thinking:

The new sciences tell us that instead of being created as perfect beings, humans have all these centuries been slowly and slowly evolving from primitive people who lived in holes and caves, and were often cannibals, to the carpenter's son from Nazareth who worshipped his heavenly Father in spirit and in truth and died with that prayer on His lips that His Father would forgive those that tortured and killed Him.

But how do scientists know all this? people will ask. They read it in the cliffs and rocks; and in the petrified remains of mammals and plant, and we know that these stones do not lie.

There is something else that has caught the fancy of the human mind. It is that people are paying attention to other religions older than Christianity and comparing them, and then see that nowhere in the Universe does God not reveal Himself.

Sometimes we are accused that these new ideas deny a belief in God. Yes, they do deny a belief in a cruel, angry, punishing God, that is true, the God that cruelly punishes innocent children. It is worthy of praise to deny these ideas.

But the God we have discovered is much more glorious and noble than the Old, more so than words can describe. But Jesus described Him best when He said, "God is a Spirit and those that worship Him must worship Him in Spirit and in Truth.... Never before have we had equal reason to say, 'I believe in God', as we do now, for now we have the knowledge to know the universe fully which is the dwelling place of the eternal spirit." 7

Some of this same optimism is reflected in her parting words to the congregation when after her final sermon they honored

her and presented her with two books of Whitman's poety and
Sir Edward Arnold's **Light of the Sea:**

> Wc have learned to let go of the childish ideas of
> orthodoxy and in its place we have nurtured the
> growing faith of free thought. This magnificent age
> of reason that influenced and still influences nations
> has reached us, and it is our hope that it will
> continue with us further and further until we reach
> the promised land where the rewards await those
> wise and good who have sown the good seed.

Several years later in a letter to her stepdaughter she
expressed another aspect of her religious philosophy in a very
personal way:

> So long as I can be of use in the world I am
> comparatively happy. The change which we call
> 'death' has no longer any terrors for me, and when
> my loved ones pass on I do not mourn for them as I
> once did. They have only passed through the change
> that is common to all humanity and which I regard
> as birth into a higher condition of life. I, too, am
> nearing the port and
> > More homelike seems the great beyond
> > Since they have entered there
> > To follow them were not so hard
> > Wherever they may fare.
>
> author?

---

1. Dr. Rögnvaldur Pétursson was minister of the Icelandic Unitarian Church in Winnipeg 1903-1909 and 1915-1922. He was a Unitarian Field Secretary 1912-1928 and 1935-40. He was not related to Björn Pétursson.
2. McCaine to Reynolds, June 24, 1888. A.U.A. letterbooks.
3. McCaine. (source not accessible to editor).
4. McCaine to Reynolds, Dec. 2, 1886. A.U.A. letterbooks.
5. McCaine to Reynolds, June 24, 1888. A.U.A. letterbooks.
6. McCaine to Reynolds, Sept. 25, 1888. A.U.A. letterbooks.
7. Obviously extracted from one of Jennie M. Petursson's sermons

Chapter 7

The First Icelandic Unitarian Church of Winnipeg

The seven years following the death of Björn Pétursson were, except for Magnús Skaptason's first two years in Winnipeg, not only difficult, but quieter and less challenging. It appears from the evidence that among the Lutherans only two or three new congregations were organized between 1895 and 1900. Undoubtedly both groups were affected by the depression of the middle Nineties which brought abject poverty in which mere physical survival was the highest priority.

It would, of course, be hard to match the influence and energy of the ferment which operated from 1885-1895. In 1885 the Icelandic Lutheran synod was organized, but right on the heels of this event, the reaction to the orthodoxy arose not only in one form, or from one source, but in at least three. J.P. Solmundsson, writing in 1904, sees the common antecedent in German rationalism which had considerable influence on Icelanders. He notes three manifestations or "streams": 1) from Robert Ingersoll, 2) from Kristofer Janson and the A.U.A., and 3) from the synod itself.

My conclusions, on the driving forces as one would infer from my previous statements, vary from Solmundsson's only in detail. In place of Ingersoll, I would place the whole free religious movment (B.F. Underwood and the like) which ranged from free thought to moderate or reinterpreted liberal Unitarian theism. Secondly, I would only reverse the order and place Jennie McCaine, the A.U.A., T.B. Forbush, and Kristofer Janson in that order. And lastly, I would be more specific and trace that stream to the liberal wing of the State Lutheran Church in Iceland, which was moderate, to say the least, on the confessions.

By the middle of the Nineties, many changes had occurred. The North Dakota Cultural Society had disbanded and its members were dispersed; and the free religious dimension was diminished at a time when it became a very weak movement in the United States. Björn Pétursson died in late 1893. Jennie McCaine Peterson left for St. Paul and then New England. Jón Ólafsson,* the gadfly intellectual, left Winnipeg, almost in disgrace, for Chicago. This meant that the "American-Icelandic" foundations in Winnipeg were largely ended. T.B. Forbush went to Memphis, and no one from the A.U.A. really replaced him. Magnús Skaptason left New Iceland where he was an undisputed leader spiritual, intellectual, and organizational, and came to Winnipeg with his strong liberal Christian bias, albeit anti-Lutheran.

When Magnús Skaptason moved from Gimli to Winnipeg, he had already begun publishing a periodical. Named **Dagsbrún** (The Dawn), it was a small 16-page monthly journal with an avowedly liberal-religious purpose in its editorial policy. In it appeared sermons composed by Björn Pétursson as well as original articles and sermons by Magnús Skaptason. Some of its articles were translations.

Financial difficulties due to a lack of subscribers ended its publication after four years, but the articles which were published provide a very valuable part of the documentation of early Icelandic religious liberalism.

The poverty among Icelanders as well as his own was Björn Pétursson's main handicap in his work. On the other hand, travel to Winnipeg (or Minneapolis) was simple: He was retired

---

*Jón Ólafson, brother-in-law to Björn Pétursson was a free-thinking intellectual who had edited one of the Icelandic papers in Winnipeg.

and thus free to come and go at will, and he lived close to the railroad.

Björn Pétursson began his "missionary" work in 1887, with the help of Kristofer Janson and his "pamphlet fund". 1 Early in April he was in Winnipeg preparing to lecture on Unitarianism and to distribute printed translations of some of Janson's pamphlets. 2

By October 1887, Pétursson had been to Winnipeg for a two-month stay. Because the people he sought to reach — that is the unchurched Icelanders — were "scattered all over the vast city, ... I had to content myself with small audiences in private houses here and there." 3 The enthusiasm was apparently less than overwhelming, but he persisted and lectured and discussed wherever he could get even a small audience. An example of his thought and themes is expressed in his report of December 1887. Apparently, one of his hopes from the beginning was to bring Jochumsson west, and he shared this dream with Janson (1887). 4

This hope became dimmer for Pétursson in 1888 as recorded in a letter to Reynolds in which he discusses Jochumsson's failing health:

> ....He is anyhow no match for the young, active and energetic Luth. minister here.... 5

Mr. Pétursson continued his missionary efforts through 1889 in much the same fashion as it did in 1888 and 1887: spending time in Winnipeg where he held a number of public meetings; visiting and preaching in Pembina County; and making a trip to Lyon County. One of the highlights for him came in October 1888 when he attended the 2nd annual meeting of the Minnesota Unitarian Conference in St. Cloud, where he met both Jennie McCaine and the Rev. Grindall Reynolds.

The summer of 1889 appears to have been his most successful one in Winnipeg. He reports to Mr. Reynolds (July 31, 1889): "Now I have everywhere (in 3 different places) had full house (100-300)." 6 This positive response caused some of "my liberal friends to want me to make my home here, and continue my work." He did return in the fall to his North Dakota home but by late November he was back in Winnipeg as reported in

Lögberg, and planning to settle there. The following year, March 11, 1890, he was married to Jennie E. McCaine — his original sponsor and supporter, by the Lutheran minister, the Rev. Jón Bjarnason. This is the beginning of the organization of Unitarianism in Winnipeg. Up to this point Pétursson had been a "travelling missioner" to use his term.

When Jennie McCaine married Björn Pétursson she very definitely became a part of the Icelandic Mission in Winnipeg. In the summer of 1890, T.B. Forbush made his initial trip to Winnipeg. He reported:

> I am not quite certain about that movement yet but I think it has promise enough to be worth fostering, and I shall recommend that it be continued at least through the year. By that time the results will be more manifest. But the results if good will be largely the result of Mrs. P's push and energy. I have more faith in her than in him. [7]

Mr. Pétursson was frequently in poor health, but then Jennie M. Pétursson was fully as much involved in his ministry as he. She preached from time to time — in English, of course, as early as 1892 and during his illness in the summer of 1893 she preached every Sunday. After his death, she served as minister and preached about half the time. But she left Winnipeg some nine months later, July 5, 1894.

T.B Forbush who of all A.U.A. people knew the Pétursson's and the Winnipeg church best, considers Mrs. "Peterson" the dominant influence in that ministry.

The First Icelandic Unitarian Society of Winnipeg was organized February 1, 1891. The Péturssons had been working toward this end for more than a year. Services and meeting had been held in different places in the city, but probably most often in the "Icelandic Hall." The book that contains the original constitution and minutes of annual meetings is entitled: **The Major Articles of Belief, Bylaws and Minutes of the First Icelandic Unitarian Society in Winnipeg.*** The first pages of the book contain "The Main Belief upon Which Unitarians Generally Agree." This is the only portion which is

*See Appendix C

definitely in Björn Pétursson's handwriting. There are eleven "articles of faith" — about God; Jesus Christ; the Holy Spirit; Humanity; Eternal Life; Resurrection; Heaven and Hell; Prayer; Church Practices; the Bible and the Devil. They are followed with a summary paragraph :

> Since we the undersigned are convinced that the Christendom represented by the Lutheran, is out of joint, archaic and in some ways dangerous, we have decided to do whtever we can to establish a free Unitarian congregation among our fellow countrymen in Winnipeg; a Christian church built on that Unitarian foundation that is set forth in the eleven articles preceding, in the spirit of Jesus of Nazareth and in harmony with healthy reason and conscience. 8

There follow 36 signatures.

The constitution with 14 articles ensues with the purpose being, "In truth and in the spirit of Jesus of Nazareth we unite for the service of God and men."

The list of chartered members is then recorded — there were 60 — of which only 24 signed the statement of beliefs. There are discrepancies: Thirty-six charter members did not sign the statement of beliefs, and 13 who signed the statement of beliefs are not recorded as charter members.

Thus with these preambles the church was organized. A three-member executive was elected — J.E. Eldon (chairman), S. Austmann, and Björn Anderson. They appointed a treasurer, Benedikt Pétursson and secretary, Kristmundur Sæmundsson.

At the seond annual meeting, January 30, 1982, forty-four members are reported. Jón Ólafsson became the chairman. It was at this meeting that the first discussion came up about the purchase of two lots on the corner of Nena and McWilliams — which had a price tag of $400. Mrs. Pétursson advised that she had been sent $100 for the support of the "mission", and a letter from Mr. Forbush was read assuring the congregation of a grant to build a meeting house. Pledges were solicited at the meeting for a total of $34 from nine families. The meeting then voted to authorize the purchase of these lots. This is further documented by Mr. Forbush in a letter to Mr. Reynolds (Feb. 19, 1892):

> I have excellent reports from Manitoba. The Winnipeg folk have bought a lot, paid $100 down and obligated themselves to pay the other $300.00 in two years. 9

The records show that several special meetings were held in 1892 regarding the purchase of the lots, raising money, and building a meeting house. At an executive meeting on November 5, 1892, it was reported that Mr. Forbush had collected $1,000 for the building. They apparently immediately sought bids, and began construction, for on December 5, 1892 Mr. Forbush stated: "The Icelandic chapel is under roof and they hope to have if finished by January 1st." 10 The congregation indeed took over the building on Christmas day 1892.

There is no doubt that T.B. Forbush, Western secretary of the A.U.A. was a significant factor in the initial success of the church in Winnipeg. There is occasional mention of Pétursson and the Winnipeg church in the pages of Unity, the magazine of the Western Unitarian Conference; and in the 1891-1892 of the WUC Yearbook the First Icelandic Unitarian Church of Winnipeg is listed.

It was T.B. Forbush (1832-98) who supported the grants and raised money for the building, but little information about him is available. He has been given only a footnote in G.W. Cooke's, **Unitarianism in America;** he does not have an entry in Eliot's **Herald of the liberal Faith.** Only Dr. Lyttle in **Freedom Moves West** gives a limited picture of this man. In the Western Unitarian struggles of the 1860's and 1870's, Forbush is lined up with those "moderate radicals" who recognize that the Unitarianism of the West is not the Christianity of Eastern Unitarianism. Lyttle characterizes his type as "intellectually radical but ecclesiastically conservative." He held "that the Conference should surrender its missionary work to the A.U.A.", and was appointed Western Superintendent. 11 The best Lyttle can say of him: "The chief accomplishment of Forbush was the formation, in 1880, of the Rocky Mountain

Conference of nine churches." Or again: "Forbush established an A.U.A. office in Chicago, but its lack of activities contrasted dismally with the busy cheerful rooms of the Conference in the Loop." 12

1. Janson to Reynolds, Feb. 24, 1887. A.U.A. letterbooks.
2. Janson to Reynolds, Apr. 2, 1887. A.U.A. letterbooks.
3. Peterson to Reynolds, Dec. 31, 1887. A.U.A. letterbooks.
4. Janson to Reynolds, June 8, 1887. A.U.A. letterbooks.
5. Peterson to Reynolds, Sept. 30, 1888. A.U.A. letterbooks.
6. Peterson to Reynolds, July 30, 1889. A.U.A. letterbooks.
7. T.B. Forbush to Reynolds, July 7, 1890. A.U.A. letterbooks.
8. See Appendix C.
9. Forbush to Reynolds, Feb. 19, 1892. A.U.A. letterbooks.
10. Forbush to Reynolds, Dec. 5, 1892. A.U.A. letterbooks.
11. Charles H. Lyttle, **Freedom Moves West** (Boston, 1952), pp. 210, 211.
12. Ibid.

Chapter 8

"Universalism" in New Iceland — Magnús J. Skaptason and The Break with Orthodox Lutheranism

"Our best destiny is to imagine who and what, and that we are. The greatest tragedy that can befall us is to go unimagined." [1]

Magnús Skaptason preached an 'Easter' sermon that spring (1891) beginning at the north end of the line of churches in New Iceland, and proceeding southward, he gave the same sermon at the other churches, presumably at Riverton, Hnausa,and Arnes. But when he reached Gimli, bedlam had broken loose and the church there had been padlocked against him. In this sermon, he denied the doctrines of hell and eternal punishment and other kindred beliefs. And the battle was on. [2]

There is currently a great interest in religious thinking in the telling of stories for in this way our place and meaning in the scheme of things, particularly the meaning, are rooted and given some life. Says James B. Wiggins, "A story of real importance is not so much a presentation as an invitation. It presents a realm of experience accessible through the imagination and invites participation in imaginative responses to reality."

One can easily sense that there is a story in and about Magnús Skaptason. In fact, there are many stories that can probably fully as well instruct and inform us about Skaptason's role in New Icelnd religion, as a detailing of the events. Some may be purely aprocryphal, such as the one I heard Guttormur J. Guttormsson[3] tell, namely, that Skaptason had the habit of putting pepper in his coffee. Many of his parishioners copied this eccentric habit, and they were the ones who supported him.

I approach this presentation* with some concern to assure that, in sifting through the accounts of this period and in establishing the historical sequence of events and looking at the data, I do not diminish the stories, or the story.

Let me just illustrate. I have nowhere found that the sermon to which Kristjánsson refers was just an Easter sermon nor that it was given anywhere on Easter Sunday. But it was given during Lent including Palm Sunday. This detail in one sense is really not important in getting an understanding of the dynamics. In another, it does matter if one seeks historical accuracy. But on with the account:

Magnús Ólafur Jósefsson was born in the north of Iceland February 4, 1850, the son of Jósef Skaftason,[4] a physician. We know he was vaccinated in 1854. Magnús headed directly on to the educational path. He graduated from the academy in Reykjavik in 1870 and went on to the School for the Ministry. His academic performance appears to have been just a little above passing. He graduated on Aug. 26, 1874, received his first settlement 2 days later, and was ordained the following spring. He was married in 1876.

For 13 years he served churches in Iceland, but in 1887 he emigrated to Canada with his family and took on the New Iceland circuit of Lutheran churches.

This circuit included 6 parishes (Mikley or Hecla, Riverton, Hnausa, Arnes, Gimli, and Willow Point). The Lutheran periodical, **Sameining,** welcomed his arrival.

He, like many other immigrants, changed his name to conform to the New World. He took his father's name Skaftason as his "family" name, retaining "J." as a 2nd initial, but dropping the "Ó". He spent the first winter at Riverton. The following spring he moved to Hnausa before it had that name. He gave his homestead the name, "Bjarkastaðir" but changed it to "Hnausa" 2 years later. In 1889 he petitioned

* Presentation of a lecture in the 1981 Minns series.

successfully for a post office to be established in his home. From it the present community of Hnausa got its name.

The records of these early congregations are only in part extant viz. Hnausa (Breiðavík) (Wide Bay) and Riverton (Bræðra) (Brotherly). We must first recognize the abject poverty of these pioneers. Several of the congregations met in community buildings which doubled also as schools. One entry in the minutes of the Hnausa church in 1888 will illustrate further the poverty. The board discussed the need for more regular communion, and since the wafers were on hand, moved and adopted "that 1 quart of communion wine be purchased, and that the Ladies Aid be asked to loan $1.00 for this purchase."

The first indication of recorded dissent or dissatisfaction is found in the minutes of the Annual Meeting of the Hnausa Church on January 20, 1881:

> 5. Ministry: The president informed men that the minister Rev. Magnús J. Skaftason had resigned, and he (the president) wished to get members' opinions now whether it was not their wish to continue his ministry. All who spoke stated that they did not want him to leave, except Magnús Jónasson who said he did not favor his continuing; that he disliked his sermon on New Years Eve, but that he disputed the doctrine of eternal damnation; that he put more emphasis on the works of love than upon faith, which he considered that a Lutheran minister should not do. Others said they found it an advantage that he was liberal in his beliefs. The minister said he could not serve a congregation that required him to preach eternal damnation. Moved: "That the meeting requests that the Rev. Magnus J. Skaftason continue as minister. Passed: 11 votes to 1."

The arrangement was that Skaptason, in serving the circuit, was called by the circuit which was composed of delegates from the six congregations. The annual meeting of this joint board was scheduled for March 31st 1891 at Gimli, at which time the main agenda was to negotiate a new contract.

Skaptason's dissent thus began about the first of the year. Undoubtedly, the New Year's sermon 5 was preached throughout the parish, but available records do not indicate whether subsequent sermons also revealed his doubts. The rumblings of the dissent reached the Synod President, the Reverend Jón Bjarnason, in Winnipeg in early March, 1891. But being in poor health, he was unable to travel to New Iceland to look into the matter. Instead, he dispatched two members of the Synod Board in his stead, namely Rev. Hafsteinn Pétursson, who was then serving the "Argyle" parish in the Glenboro-Baldur area, and the Treasurer, Árni Friðriksson. The most detailed account of the events leads immediately to Magnús Skaptason's split with the Synod. This appears in a report that Hafsteinn Pétursson wrote in **Lögberg** April 8, 1891. The immediate doctrinal issue seems to have been the doctrine of Original Sin, although other articles of the Augsburg Confession gave Skaptason problems. And H. Pétursson's mission was to "lead Skaftason back to his senses. It is our Christian brotherly obligation to point out to Magnús the error of his ways."

These two gentlemen traveled directly to Hnausa, leaving Winnipeg on Wednesday, the 18th of March. When they met with Skaptason, "He told us clearly that he could no longer accept the doctrine of Original Sin.. He denies completely that the wages of sin are eternal punishment." He had preached a sermon to this effect already at Mikley (Hekla Island) and planned to repeat it in the rest of his churches. The churches could then choose whether they wanted him to continue as their pastor.

These two men accompanied Skaptason to Icelandic River. The following weekend and on Sunday, the 22nd of March, he preached for the congregation. I shall look at this sermon a little later, for it is extant.*

Although the accounts of H. Pétursson and Skaptason differ on some details, we know that some discussion followed, mostly controversial, and a congregational meeting was set for

*This sermon appears in Appendix D.

the following Saturday. The minutes record the debate in some detail.

The theological rumblings thus began about the first of the year. The Riverton congregation met in March 1891 when Skaptason had apparently already preached his anti-eternal-damnation sermon. After a length debate, they voted 35-6 not to renew the contract, the only one of the 6 congregations to do so. The sermon was preached at Hnausa on March 27th (Good Friday) probably at Arnes on Easter Sunday, and at Gimli March 30th, Easter Monday. (Apendix IV).

The question of what was the **essence** of the controversy expressed in the sermon is summarized in the concluding paragraph of his "break-away" sermon:

> It is contrary to my nature to want to assuage or diminish punishment for committed sins, for as I am convinced that our loving, heavenly Father has never intended anyone to be tortured in eternal damnation, so I am convinced that He must punish us for even the smallest transgression. However, the punishment is to be related to our betterment, for in that way we come closer and closer to the light of our eternal beneficent Father. Punishment is one of the Lord's plans in this world to lead souls to Himself, to peace and bliss."[6]

Thus, in the words of Kristjánsson,[7] the battle was on.

The meeting of the delegate board was held at Gimli, March 31st with representation from these congregations at (Willow Pt., Gimli, Árnes, Hnausa, Fljótshlíð, and Mikley). Missing is Icelandic River (Riverton). Two representatives were sent to Gimli to "try to lead him in the right direction" but "they were unsuccessful in proving to Rev. Magnús his spiritual errors." He resigned from the Synod on April 3rd. Four of the congregations also resigned (Hnausa, Arnes, Gimli, and Willow Point). The Synod president expressed a little consternation that neither Skaftason nor two of the congregations gave any reason for these actions and a committee was appointed which brought in recommendations with nine points:

1. Skaftason obviously preached his heretical views while still a synod minister which is contrary to the Christian spirit and the synod rules.

2. In his letter of resignation, Skaftason gives no reason, showing lack of respect for the church.

3. He has shown that not only does he deny the doctrine of eternal damnation, but also the divine revelation of holy scripture leading him to the infidel views of Unitarians, and he has preached at the Unitarian Church.

4. Only the Arnes congregation has set forth reasons for its withdrawal.

5. Hnausa and Gimli give no reason despite the fact that this is their moral and Christian duty.

6. The withdrawal of Willow Point is invalid since a portion of the congregation maintains contact with the Synod and the property belongs to this portion whether it is in the majority or not.

7. The Riverton congregation fulfilled its legal and Christian obligations in terminating the services of Skaftason.

8. Hopefully the Hecla congregation will see the light when it has received full information about Skaftason's views.

9. Whereas it is obvious that Skaftason is no longer a Lutheran minister, yet it appears that many who supported him are in their hearts still faithful to the Lutheran faith, that it is the prayerful advice to all such persons that they do not allow themselves to be led from their faith.

Letters ensued, pro and con, in the pages of both **Lögberg** and **Heimskringla.** the Synod president as editor of **Sameining** published a scathing comment about the moral character of Skaftason, suggesting that wine was his downfall, leading him to fraternize with the scum of society. He is accused of keeping secret from his New Iceland congregations his contacts with the American Unitarian Association.   His first letter, Sept. 11, 1891,requests copies of the works of Channing. His next letter refers to a $200 grant that he has been voted by the A.U.A.

board. But the explanation for this quick support of a
Universalist Christian is clarified in the following extract from
a Forbush letter to A.U.A. Secretary Reynolds. (June 19, 1891)
after a trip to Winnipeg:

> I was so fortunate as to meet Rev. Magnús
> Skaptason. He is the man up on the west side of
> Lake Winnipeg who has lately renounced
> Lutheranism. He was pastor of seven churches
> scattered along a 60 mile coast of Lake Winnipeg.
> He was educated in Iceland and entered the ministry
> there. He was a classmate of Oalfson [sic],
> Peterson's brother-in-law and thus was brought in
> contact with Peterson and liberal views of religion.
> Of his seven churches, five have followed him away
> from Lutheranism, one is divided with the majority
> in his favor, one adheres to the old church. The
> territory he covers is called New Iceland. It has
> 2,300 Icelandic inhabitants; of these 2,000 adhere to
> Mr. Skaptason. His home is at Gimli high up on the
> west coast of Lake Winnipeg. 8 The remaining
> churches, or perhaps the churches that remained
> with Skaptason, organized themselves as the
> Icelandic Free Church Association of America.

1. Source not identified. Ed.
2. Rev. Albert E. Kristjánson in a letter to the author Feb. 6, 1961.
3. A prominent Icelandic Canadian poet, contemporary of Magnús Skaptason.
4. Note the change from the Icelandic patronymic "Jósefson" to the adapted family
surname, "Skaftason" later "Skaptason", a common practice among Icelandic settlers in
North America. The original Icelandic spelling is "Skaftason", but in North America it was
changed to "Skaptason".
5. Not to be confused with the "Breakaway" (sermon which appears in translation in
Appendix D.
6. Translated by the author from the original Icelandic.
7. See note 2 (above).
8. Forbush to Reynolds, June 19, 1891. A.U.A. letterbooks.

Chapter 9

Depressions, Doubts and Indecisions, 1895 - 1900*

The late 1800's and the early 1900's are the so-called "doubtful years", because the author saw them as a critical period for the survival of organized Unitarianism in Winnipeg and the Icelandic settlements in rural Manitoba. Several reasons are given for the arrested development of the movement. It was a period of economic depression which placed many of the immigrants in a state of abject poverty.Mere physical survival had to be given priority over participation in cultural and spiritual affairs. Another reason is given as the shortage of qualified religious leaders to serve in the widely-scattered settlements. Several prominent Unitarian laypersons had moved from Winnipeg to other locations.

---

*Editor's Note: The author's manuscript for this chapter was never written. However, the tape recording of Lecture 6 of the Minns lectures he delivered in Manitoba is extant. I have reviewed this recording and gleaned from it such material as can be related to the chapter title, this being the only available material for the purpose.

The content of the tape has been edited with a view to deletion of "asides", repetitions, and other irrelevancies which formed portions of the lecture, but were probably not intended for inclusion in this part of the book. Some of the material submitted here is condensed and slightly reworded, but this has been done without altering meaning or tone. Much of it appears as a verbatim transcription from the tape recording.   GEB

The Péturssons, Björn and Jennie, were not replaced until around 1900 when Rev. Magnús Skaptason took over the Winnipeg congregation. Even so, Winnipeg's gain was New Iceland's loss, for Skaptason was not readily replaced in the rural area, and his commitments in Winnipeg made it difficult for him to serve also his former congregations except on a part-time basis. The Icelandic congregations were deprived of the benevolent assistance of T.B. Forbush, Western Secretary of the A.U.A., when he was transferred from comparatively nearby Chicago to Memphis, Tennessee in 1897.

Special tribute should be paid to the perseverence of Magnús Skaptason. His periodical, **Dagsbrún** (The Dawn), documented much of the history of the beginnings of religious liberalism among the Icelanders. Incidentally, Skaptason came to the Winnipeg congregation with the understanding that he would continue to serve the New Iceland parish. Actually, he managed to visit it four or five times per year as well as making calls at Selkirk, Manitoba where he had a few followers

In Winnipeg, Skaptason succeeded in reviving the flagging interest in the affairs of the church, it having diminished since the resignation of Jennie M. Pétursson in 1893. Membership increased from 16 to 76 in two years of Skaptason's tenure. Other evidence of growth and progress appears in Rev. Skaptason's report of the re-establishment of the Sunday school in 1895, since it had been discontinued in the later years of Pétursson. It should be noted that one of the Sunday school teachers was Dr. Magnús Halldórsson, a Winnipeg physician who chanced to be a grand-nephew of Magnús Eiríksson (Chapter 2). The other teachers were Rev. Skaptason, Sveinn Thorvaldsson, and S. Jóhansson.

It is related that one of the factors which inhibited the growth of Unitarianism was discrimination practiced by the orthodox members of the Icelandic community in Winnipeg. According to T.B. Forbush:

> The (Unitarian) church was located across the street from the larger First Lutheran (Icelandic) Church. I got the impression (on my 1896 visit) that...many people on their way to the Unitarian Church, if they met certain people on the street, would not want to

admit where they were going, and would duck into the Lutheran Church across the street.

Magnús Skaptason corroborated this impression:

> When I came from the settlement in Winnipeg,... prejudices against the Unitarians were so strong that they (some of them) had not the courage to avow the Unitarian faith..The Unitarian name was both hated and despised. Whenever a man avowed himself to be a Unitarian, he was persecuted. If he was a laborer, nobody would give him work. If he was a mechanic, it was the same. If he was a merchant or some kind of dealer, he could not get any customers.

The missionary zeal of **Magnús Skaptason** most certainly deserves applause for his attempts to proselytize in the North Dakota settlements — at the same time as he was serving the Winnipeg and New Iceland churches. He spent six weeks one summer in Dakota, preaching to congregations numbering up to 60. Apparently, however, although his talks were popular, only a very few of his hearers went so far as to formally accept Unitarianism. Possibly their exposure to it was for too short a time — or they felt uncomfortable with the thought of pulling away from the Lutheran majority.

In Winnipeg, the question arose whether Magnús Skaptason's ultimate successor would be expected to preach in Icelandic or in English. A letter from some members of the congregation to the A.U.A. indicated, in 1899:

> ...We have been unable to obtain any Icelander to educate for the ministry...and think it would be advisable to try to organize a Unitarian Church here from **all sources.** As far as the nationality is concerned,...the Icelandic members of the present congregation would join in such a movement. ı

Prior to this time, however, (in 1895), it is recorded that:

Magnús Skaptason had brought a young man to
meet Mr. Forbush to have an interview about
whether he might be a candidate to go to Meadville.
And this was Mr. (Jóhann) Solmundsson...From
1895 there would be another three years (before) he
finally went to Meadville.

Editor's note: Emil Gudmundson's manuscript notes
concerning Mr. Solmundsson have not been located to date.
However, information has been supplied by Solmundsson's
surviving daughter, Thorbjörg Davidson of Winnipeg. Her
father did in fact attend Meadville Theological School. 2
     He served The Winnipeg congregation from 1902 to 1903,
succeeding Skaptason. He then served the congregation in
Gimli, which he had helped to organize, until 1910.

---

1. Frederick Swanson to Samuel A. Eliot, Jan. 31, 1899. A.U.A. letterbooks.
2. See biographical note on Johann P. Solmundsson in Appendix J.

Chapter 10

Anticipating The Twentieth Century *

The Icelandic Conference of Unitarian Churches in North America was organized at Gimli in 1901. Some very interesting things were written about its beginnings by Franklin C. Southworth (who later became president of Meadville Theological School) in his capacity as Secretary for the Western Unitarian Conference, and the A.U.A. representative in the Midwest as well. He came from Chicago for this meeting. He wrote:

> I have just returned from what may be safely characterized as the northermost Unitarian conference which has ever been held in the Western Hemisphere.

Then he goes on into the history of that and tells about coming up to the conference:

> In order to reach Gimli, it was necessary to take the Canadian Pacific Railroad from Winnipeg to

*From the edited notes for Lecture 6 in the 1981 Minns Lecture Series.

Selkirk. From there we embarked, on the morning
of June 15th, a party of about 15, in a small
sailboat. A favoring breeze took us 22 miles in less
than five hours to the mouth of the Red River. Then
the wind died down for a time and when it rose
again it was dead ahead. We spent the rest of the
day beating back and forth as the force of the wind
increased and finally at half past 10 in the evening,
to our great joy, succeeded in rounding Willow
Point and beholding the lights of Gimli.

(Now, this would have indicated that it was some eight hours
that they were there.)

A violent rain had set in by that time, and as we
neared the shore, thunder and lightning made an
interesting scene. I could almost imagine myself
under the power of Thor and Odin and among a
group of Norse Vikings such as roved the seas a
thousand years ago. About 11:00 o'clock at night we
disembarked and, as Gimli was still destitute of
sidewalks, we waded through the mud to our
lodging place where we were fortunate enough to
find a good supper awaiting us.

He then goes on to say that several untoward events seemed to
have conspired against the success of the meeting — and yet it
succeeded:

In the first place the season was late and the farmers
had not finished their spring work. The delegates
from North Dakota could not attend in the numbers
they wanted to. Two school teachers from Lake
Manitoba had driven 46 miles in order to get the
train for Winnipeg where they joined the party. And
for several who were present, it was long travel.

It was probable that the people from the northern settlement,
by and large, had to come on foot because there was too much
mud in places for the horses to take them.

Another difficulty in the way was the absence of a suitable place for meeting. There was an attractive village church of concrete in Gimli, built by Mr. Skaftason's congregation, when it was still in the Lutheran fold, and when the congregation became Unitarian, the church building naturally went with the Unitarians. But during the absence of a liberal minister at Gimli, another Lutheran minister made his appearance and has held the church by right of possession. When, therefore, a request was made for the use of the building for the conference, it was ruthlessly refused. A request for the use of the schoolhouse met with like refusal. Our meetings were, therefore, held in a portion of a recently erected hotel. The building was not finished and, during the rainstorms which visited the conference from time to time, we were obliged to shift our position occasionally in order to keep dry.

The first officers of the Icelandic Unitarian Association were: President, Rev. Magnús Skaptason, Vice-President, Skapti Brynjólfssen; Secretary, Thorvaldur Thorvaldsson, Treasurer; Fred Swanson; Mission Superintendent, Einar Ólafsson. The trustees were S. Johnson from Mountain and S. Sigbjörnsson of Arnes. And then the plans were made for the starting of an Icelandic Unitarian quarterly which was the beginnings of **Heimir.** I might comment, however, that in the interregnum there was a journal put out by Solmundsson with two issues, called **Nýa Dagsbrún.** I In the intervening years in the late 1890's Magnús Skaptason attempted to start another journal which he called **Lýsing.** 2 Four or five issues of **Lýsing** were published.

Now, about the other part of the conference: This was "done up brown". They had all the elements there even if they did not have a large attendance and much too much rain.

The session of the conference which was most interesting to me was held on the afternoon of Tuesday, June 18, when after a sermon by Mr. Skaptason eight grey-eyed and fair-skinned babies were brought to the church to be christened by the only American Unitarian Association representative present. So

Southworth had to do it. He was the only American present and was asked to do the christening of these New Iceland children, with their almost unpronounceable names. He commented as follows:

> I trembled a little when I studied the list of names which was handed to me. The first on the list came easily...Benjamin Franklin Olson.* But then when I proceeded further, I had the rest of the names like Hrafnkell, Steinthor, Hjalti...

(I'm sure he didn't pronounce them in the pure Icelandic way!)

> I had a lurking fear that the parents would not recognize their offspring by the terms in which they were being addressed.

One of the most interesting featues of the conference, to me, was the fact that it was a conference of men. There has sometimes been, in the past, a noticeable absence of the masculine element in our Unitarian meetings. That was not the case at Gimli. The delegates were not only all men, but with one or two exceptions, were all **young** men. And it was noted over and over again that the people who came to the Unitarian meetings at the Unitarian churches, the church of Winnipeg and the churches in New Iceland at that period, were young men. However, I would have to say from the list of members, there was almost an equal number, not quite but almost, of men and women in those congregations. It was fairly evenly divided.

These were hard years and I think there was no assurance at any given time that the movement would continue. Having but one minister, serving the congregation in the largest city where the largest number of his countrymen lived, and being the missionary, an active missionary, to all the other areas, especially New Iceland and North Dakota, was a great task. A number of these were doubtful years. One has to conclude that it took an unusual person of great determination, of strength,

*Olson, several years later, was Emil Gudmundson's high school teacher at Lundar, Manitoba.

vigor, and energy to keep that movement alive, and that person was Magnús Skaptason.

I'm interested in the label that Albert Kristjánsson put on the two founders. He said if you were to compare Björn Pétursson and Magnús Skaptason to two of the founding members and early leaders of Unitarianism, you would have to conclude that Björn Pétursson was like Theodore Parker[3], one who was constantly seeking controversy and the like, while Magnús Skaptason who was steady, was more like William E. Channing.[4] And I think it is apt to conclude this series * by attributing the spirit of Channing to Magnús Skaptason a liberal Christian who was going to keep the tradition even as he ventured forth on fulfilling the mission of a liberated religion for his countrymen.

1. **Nýa Dagsbrún** (New Dawn) to replace Magnús Skaptason's **Dagsbrún** (Dawn) which had been discontinued because of lack of funds.
2. **Lýsing** (Enlightenment). Note the symbolism of the names of these publications. Ed.
3. Theodore Parker (1810-60). American Unitarian clergyman, was known for his rationalistic views on religion.
4. William Ellery Channing (1780-1842). American Unitarian clergyman, was an eloquent preacher. While he opposed the teaching of dogma, he tried to avoid ecclesiastical quarrels.

GEB

*The 1981 Minns Lectures.

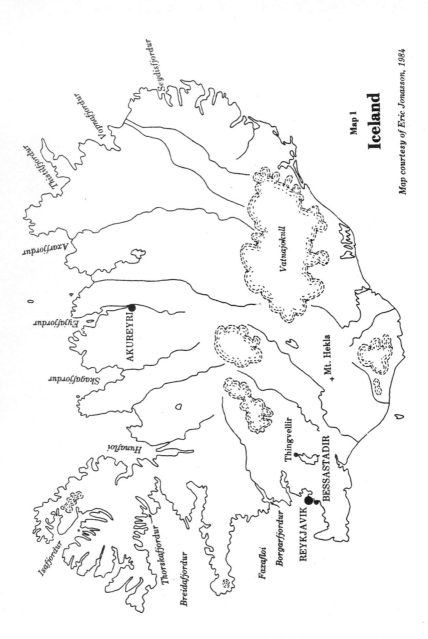

Map 1
Iceland

Map courtesy of Eric Jonasson, 1984

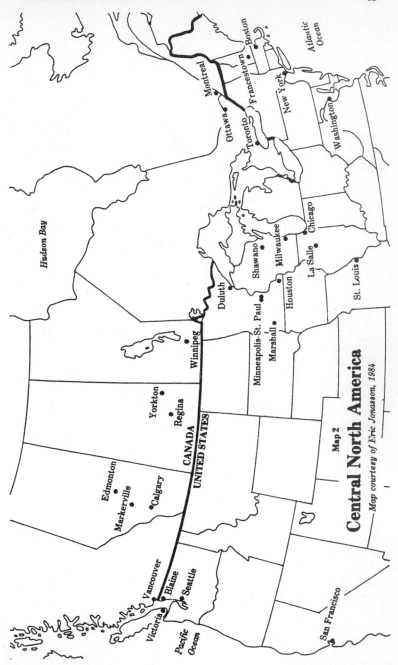

Central North America

— *Map courtesy of Eric Jonasson, 1984*

Map 2

Hudson Bay

Atlantic Ocean

Boston
Francestown
New York
Washington
Montreal
Ottawa
Toronto
Chicago
Milwaukee
Shawano
La Salle
St. Louis
Duluth
Houston
Minneapolis-St. Paul
Marshall
Winnipeg
Yorkton
Regina
CANADA
UNITED STATES
Edmonton
Markerville
Calgary
Vancouver
Blaine
Seattle
Victoria
San Francisco
Pacific Ocean

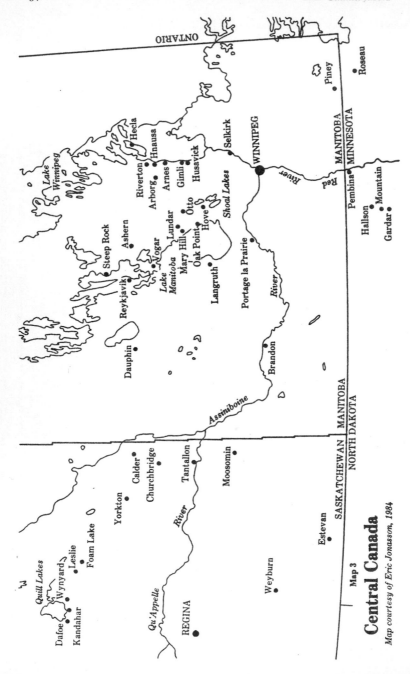

Central Canada

Map courtesy of Eric Jonasson, 1984

Map 3

Magnús Eiríksson

Matthías Jochumsson

Björn Pétursson   Stephan G. Stephansson

Kristofer Janson
(Norwegian-American Historical Assn.)

First Federated Church of Riverton

T.B. Forbush

First Federated Church of Gimli

Jennie McCaine Peterson

Winnipeg Unitarian Church

Arnes Unitarian Church, at Hnausa

Magnús J. Skaptason

Hecla Church, 1890

Hecla Church, 1982

Barbara R. and V. Emil Gudmundson, 1982
(David Loehr)

Arborg Unitarian Church

Appendix A

Magnús Eiríksson Bibliography

Works in Danish:

Om Baptister og Barnedarb, 1844 (About Baptists and Child Christening), at *U. of Manitoba, Harvard, Cornell*

Tro, Overtro, Vantro 1846 (Faith, Fanaticism and Unbelief), at *Harvard*

Dr. Martensens trykte moralske Paragrapher, 1846 (Dr. Martensen's printed moral essays), at *Harvard, Cornell*

Spekulativ Rettroenhed, 1849 (Speculative Orthodoxy), at *Harvard*

Den nydanske Theologies Cardinaldyder, 1850 (The New Danish Theologies' Cardinal Virtues), at *Harvard, Cornell*

Er Troen et Paradox? 1850, 215 pp. (Is Belief a Paradox?), at *Northwestern*

Breve til Clara Raphael 1851, (Letter to Clara Raphael)

Er Johannes Evangelist et apostloisk og aegte Evangelium oger dets Laere on Guds Menneskvorden en sand of christelig Laere?, 1863 (Is John the Evangelist an apostolic and real gospel and is his teaching about God becoming human — a true Christian teaching?), at *Harvard, Cornell*

Hvem Har Ret: Grundtvigianerne eller deres Modstandere og Hvad har Christus befalet on Daaben? 1863 (Who is Right...), at *Cornell*

Gud og Reformatoren, 1866 (God and the Reformation)

On Ronnens Virking, 1870, 70 pp. (About the Workings of Prayer), at *Harvard, Cornell*

Kunne vi elske Naesten sam os selv 1870, 115 pp. (Can we love our neighbor as ourselves?), at *Harvard, Cornell, Northwestern*

Paulus og Christus, 1871 (Paul and Christ), at *Harvard, Cornell*

Joder og Christne, 1873, 312 pp. (Jew and Christian), at *New York Public*

Herr A. Pedrin og Christendommen, 1874, 16 pp. (Mr. A. Pedrin and Christendom), at *Harvard*

Min Forfattervirksomhed (Flyvende Blade), 1875

Works in Icelandic

Jóhannesar guðspjall og lærdómur kirkjunnar um Guð, 1865 (The Gospel of John and the church's teachings about God), at *U. of Manitoba, Cornell*

Nokkrar sannanir, "katólsku prestanna í Reykjavík" fyrir guðdómi Jesús Krists, 1868 (Some proofs of the Catholic priests in Reykjavik about the deity of Jesus Christ), at *U. of Manitoba, Cornell*

Svar upp á "Hálfyrði prestsins í Þjóðólfi", 1866

Works by others

See Eiríkur Albertsson, **Magnús Eiríksson, Guðfræði hans og Trúarlíf** (Magnús Eiríksson, His Theology and Religious Life), 1938, at *U. of Manitoba*

See also Harvard/Meadville lectures by Prof. Águst Bjarnason, and "Um Magnús Eiríksson", **Skirnir,** 1924, Vol. 98, pp. 39-73

Appendix B

Purpose, Membership and By-Laws of The Icelandic Cultural Society

HUMANITY, RESEARCH, FREEDOM

The objectives of this organization are to support and promote culture and ethics, that ethics and that faith which is based upon experience, knowledge and science. In place of ecclesiastical sectarianism, it seeks humanitarianism and fellowship; in place of unexamined confessions of faith, sensible and unfettered research; in place of blind faith, independent conviction; and in place of ignorance and superstition, spiritual freedom and progress upon which no fetters are placed.

By-Laws:

Article I   The name of this organization shall be The
                Icelandic Cultural Society.

Article II   The objectives of this society are stated in the
                Statement of Purpose which is appended.
                Membership is open to those are in sympathy
                with the Statement of Purpose, approve with
                their signature the By-Laws, are 16 years of age,
                and have the recommendation of the
                Membership Committee.

Article III   Each member shall pay annual dues of one
                dollar. The membership Committee can waive
                the dues for valid reasons, but especially if a
                member shall move away but wishes to retain his
                membership.

Article IV   Each member shall have full freedom of
                expression and the right to vote, but only those
                who are 21 or older shall have the right of
                election.

Article V   The annual meeting shall be held in the month of
                June, public meetings on public holidays if
                possible, and special meeting when necessary.

Article VI   The Annual Meeting elects a Board of Directors,
                approves a budget, plans for the following year,
                and conducts whatever other business may come
                before the meeting.

Article VII   Any meeting is legal which is properly called and
                at which 7 members attend, except when the
                budget is under consideration, at which time half
                the membership must be present. A majority
                shall prevail in all decisions unless otherwise
                agreed.

Article VIII   The Board shall consist of the president,
                treasurer, secretary and 3 person Membership
                Committee chosen for one year, and alternates
                for each office.

Article IX   The president shall conduct meetings and call them, call special meetings if 7 members request one, and name committees which are given duties for the year.

Article X   The Treasurer shall receive all dues of members, pay all bills which are approved by the President and secretary; he shall present an annual financial report to the Annual Meeting, and other reports when requested; he shall have a record of all transactions.

Article XI   The Secretary shall take minutes of all meetings, attend to all correspondence for the Society, and shall keep for safekeeping all papers, records and books for the Society.

Article XII   The membership Committee shall approve applications for membership who apply in writing and meet the requirements of Article II. The committee shall be unanimous in their recommendations for membership of all who apply for membership. Any application must be approved by a two thirds vote.

Article XIII The Society can subdivide into departments as the need arises, which shall be under the supervision of the Board of Directors in such manner as they agree upon.

Article XIV   Membership dues shall be paid before the Annual Meeting.

Article XV   Amendments to these by-laws shall be made only at Annual Meetings.

Names of Members:

Ólaf Ólafsson	*Magnús Halldórsson*
Kristján R. Casper	*Stephan G. Stephansson*
Jón Hjalmarson	*John Guðmundsson*
Jónas Hall	*Einar Jónasson*
Bjarni Johnson	*Jacob Lindal*

S. Tryggvi Guðmundsson
Ásgeir J. Lindal
Sveinn Björnsson
S. Johnson
Magnús Brynjólfsson
Gísli Jóhanneson
Sigurður Einarsson
Gisli Sæmundsson
Jón Jónsson Hrafndal
A. Magnússon
Árni Árnason
Magnús Snowfield

Tryggvi Pálsson
S.J. Björnsson
S.B. Brynjólfsson
Bjarni Jóhannson
H. Thomson
Björn Halldórsson
Björn Pétursson
B. Blöndal
Arngrímur Jónsson
Sigfús Salómon
B. Bjarnarson

Appendix C

Constitution and By-Laws of the First Icelandic Unitarian Church of Winnipeg

~~~~~~

THE MAJOR ARTICLES OF BELIEF*

The Main Beliefs Upon Which Unitarians Generally Agree

1. About God

Unitarians believe that there is only one God, changeless, which has existed for eternity, who has created, sustained and governed all things by perfect laws which he has himself established.

They believe that He is unprovable spirit but men best reach his nature if they consider him as their all mild - almighty, all-wise, omnipotent, all-knowing heavenly father. They believe that God is prepared to forgive every sinner who repents and changes his ways; that his love is eternal and boundless, and the misery and wretchedness to which sin leads, according to God's laws is only the discipline which leads to improvement whenever the sinner so desires.

They believe that God is revealed only in his works in nature, in reason, in conscience of all men, but openly in those who have excelled in knowledge and have become leaders of mankind for the good.

2. About Jesus Christ

Unitarians believe that Jesus Christ was the Master Teacher and one of the purest of heart of men, whoever lived; that he taught us to know the path to God, and he himself trod that path with self denial and love; and he is, for this reason, rightly called Our Savior and an example for all time.

*By-laws and Minutes of the First Icelandic Unitarian Society in Winnipeg which was established February 1, 1891.

3. About the Holy Spirit

Unitarians believe that the Holy Spirit is not a person, rather represents that spiritual power of God, which He operates through his creation, humanity, in a manner like the human spirit can have and has influence on another person.

4. About Man (Humanity)

Unitarians believe that man is created in God's image, i.e., God's undying spirit resides in us, and that we are rightly called God's children — sons and daughters. They believe that the human purpose is to return to the God from whence we came, and that (we) have the potential to reach this (purpose) and that everyone attains it sooner or later, through more or less experience and trials.

They believe that each sin has its own punishment, and every good work done with honesty has its own reward. They believe that man has free will to determine his own destiny and must always therefore bear responsibility for all his works.

5. About Eternal Life

They believe that the human spirit lives forever, since it is a part of the Spirit of God, and that after death it takes on eternal progress.

6. About the Resurrection

Unitarians believe that the human spirit has its own spiritual body after death, which leaves its earthly body.

7. About Heaven and Hell

Unitarians believe that Heaven represents the sun-rich state of the human soul after death while Hell is the undesirable state.

8. About Prayer

Unitarians believe that prayer uplifts the soul to God and is necessary for those who feel the need to seek.

9. About Church Practices

They consider baptism and communion to be authentic, beautiful, and actually meaningful church practices and for that reason useful although only to those who desire that they be practiced.

10. About the Bible

Unitarians believe that the Bible is the world's most important book for Christians because it explains the history, ethics and customs of those nations from which Jesus came; likewise because it relates words and works of Jesus of Nazareth and about how his disciples understood him though the stories are faulty and unreliable.

11. About the Devil

Unitarians do not believe that there is any personal devil; rather, the name of the devil represents evil in the world in all its aspects.

Since we, the undersigned, are convinced that the Christendom the Lutheran Church promotes is out of joint, archaic, and in some ways dangerous, we have determined to do what we can to establish a free Unitarian congrgation among our fellow countrymen in Winnipeg, a Christian church built on that Unitarian foundation that is set forth in the 11 articles preceeding, in the spirit of Jesus of Nazareth, and concerned with healthy rationalism and conscience.

Björn Pétursson
F. Merrill
Rósa Indriðadóttir
Baldur E. Eldon
Friðik Sveinsson
Ó. Ólafsson
S.J. Eastman
Mr. Th. Oddson
Mrs. S. Merrill
Kristmundur Sæmundson
Sigriður Halldórsdóttir
N.M. Lambertsen
Benedict Sigurðson
Barny Johnson
Sigfús Magnússon

Sigurður Indriðasson
Páll Bergson
Kristján Jacobson
Mrs. A.M. Eldon
B. Árnason
Kristján Jónsson
B. Ólafsson
Mrs. A. Gislason
J. Runolfsson
G.O. Th. Oddson
Eiríkur Gíslason
E. Ólafsson
Sigfús B. Benediktsson
A. Bjarnason
Th. J. Mjófjörd

Benedict Pjetursson   *Steffan B. Jonsson*
J.E. Eldon   *Wm. Anderson*
Sölvi Thorsteinsson   *S. Jónsson*

ARTICLE I
The name of this society is: The 1st Icelandic Unitarian Church of Winnipeg.
ARTICLE II
The purpose of this society is: In truth and in the spirit of Jesus of Nazareth, we unite for the service of God and men.
ARTICLE III - About Worship
Worship shall be conducted with hymns and preaching. Christenings will be held in the church or in homes as requested.
ARTICLE IV
The conduct of Christening shall be as the minister and the participants agree.
ARTICLE V- The rights and duties of the society
The congregation shall call its own minister and shall make an agreement with him.
ARTICLE VI
Each member of the congregation shall as means permit contribute his/her share for all necessary expenses of the society.
ARTICLE VII
Men and women, age 15 or over will have freedom of discussion at meetings, but the right to vote shall be restricted to those aged 18 or over.
ARTICLE VIII - The Responsibility and Rights of the Preacher/Cleric
The responsibilities and rights of the preacher shall be detailed in a contract between him and the congregation.
ARTICLE IX - About Joining and Leaving
Whoever agrees with the statement of purpose and signs the membership book will be a member. The signing may be done either at a congregational meeting or at the house of the president (chair). At the following service of worship the minister shall announce the joining to the congregation and welcome the new member.

ARTICLE X

Should someone desire to remove themselves from the society, he shall inform the preacher or chairman; those who move away and live elsewhere for a year are no longer members unless special arrangments are agreed upon, and likewise those who without cause neglect their attendance or fail to support adequately the finances of the society.

ARTICLE XI - Board

In the governing board of the society are: Chair, Vice-Chair, Secretary, and Treasurer. These officers shall be elected for one year. In addition, there shall be 3 board members, one elected for 3 years, one for 2 years and one for 1 year. All these people shall be given an official letter which shall be accepted at a legally called membership meeting.

ARTICLE XII - Property

The question of property shall be decided when the need arises and if there are any.

ARTICLE XIII - Board Meetings and Annual Meeting

Meetings concerning the private business of the society shall be held monthly. Special meetings can be called by the board as the need arises. The annual meeting shall be held the last Saturday in January annually. No one can be seated without membership. The quorum at a legally called meeting shall be no less than 1/3 of the votes of the members.

Other meetings shall be held with the consent of the membership to discuss public matter and spiritual questions. At these meetings everyone is welcome.

ARTICLE XIV

This constitution shall not be amended nor anything added without a 2/3 majority vote of the membership. Each proposal for amendment shall be brought up for discussion at the preceding meeting.

Then follow a set of by-laws — summarized:

    Art. 1 - Chairman and duties
    Art. 2 - Vice Chair
    Art. 3 - Secretary
    Art. 4 - Treasurer
    Art. 5 - Trustees
    Art. 6 - Ushers

Art. 7 - Committees a) School b) Music
Art. 8 - Vacancies
Art. 9 - Agenda or Order of Business
Art. 10 - Majority Rule by ballot or voice
Art. 11 - Amendments

Then follows the list of members:

Björn Pétursson	J. E. Peterson
E. Gíslason	Valdimar Davíðsson
Jakobína Halldórsdóttir	Wm. Anderson
E. Ólafsson	Mrs. Gíslason
Mrs. Merrill	J. E. Eldon
Sigurdur Indriðason	Kristmundur Sæmundsson
Baldur E. Eldon	Regina Smith
Jón Ólafsson & family	Benedikt Pjetursson
Lára Erlendsdóttir	Guðrún` Anderson
Mrs. A. E. Eldon	Sigurbjörg Sölvadóttir
I. Merrill	Árni Thorðarsson Dahlmann
Eiríkur Davídsson	G. Larson
Björn Árnason	S. J. Austmann
W. E. Liend	S. B. Benediktsson
Ólafur Ísleifsson	Jón Sigurðsson
Ólafur Sigurðsson	Jósef Axfirðingur
H. B. Jónsson	Friðrik Sveinsson
Ólöf Bjarnardóttir	A. P. Bjarnarson
Magnús Pétursson	Jónas Magnússon
Ó. Ólafsson	S. T. Pétursson
Íngibjörg Johnson	S Thórarinsson
Íngibjörg Björnsdóttir	Stefán Jónsson
S. Johnson	Maggie Johnson
Stefán Johnson	P. Guðmundsson
Jóna Jónasdóttir	Albert Guðmundsson
Ólafur Eiríksson	B. Johnson
Jón Sigvaldason	S. Sölvason
Sigurður V. Ólafsson	Sigfús Thórarinsson
G. Ólafsson	G. Thórarinsson
Helga Jónatansdóttir	

Appendix D

The "Break-Away" Sermon of Magnús J. Skaptason

SERMON *
delivered at Gimli, March 30, 1891
by
The Rev. Magnús J. Skaptason
Gimli, Man.
Printed at the author's expense by G.M. Thompson
1892

"Go from me, you cursed,
into the eternal fire,
prepared for the devil
and his angels"

Matt. 25:41

When I was a child (in age), I remember well what fright shot through me, when I thought about the condition of the souls of the damned, and all the pains that they were to endure throughout eternity. I thought about if during the day, I dreamt about it at night, about all those endless pains, which had been described to me so dreadfully. When I matured, I began to find them slightly repulsive; I began to ask myself why an all-wise heavenly father must really punish us, his children, in this manner. Then I began to doubt whether an all-good, all-merciful Father was in reality so callous that he could not forgive his children, as earthly fathers forgive their children — something that I have seen and experienced personally. But there are no exceptions; it stood everywhere in black and white; it rang in my ears from the lips of our teachers, both lay and learned. This was being etched in my soul with indelible ink. I twisted and turned every way, as a criminal on the rack, and tried to believe that God saved the repentant sinner. But I never

*An edited version of the author's translation of Skaptason's sermon from the original Icelandic.

knew whether I was among the chosen or not; and not-
withstanding, the sinners remained a majority of the
population who had to suffer and be tormented in the eternal
fire. "Were they not God's children just as I am? Why did God
then create them?", I thought, "and why could these souls then
love the One who has in his possession the inextinguishable fire
of torment?" I tried to convince myself that this must be the
way it is, but I never understood it. When I was growing up, I
could never be really frightened of damnation, since I doubted
it more and more, until the doubt of earlier years has now
become my fullest conviction, which is continually
strengthened as my idea of God has developed and matured. In
addition, my belief in Him has become firmer and built on a
broader foundation which has also been stengthened as I have
seen his handiwork in the universe, and as I have acknowledged
His rule in the small issues as in the large. His life is present in
all existence; His love abounds before me; His omnipotence
and wisdom smile before me in every straw, hide in every idea,
and press through everything and everybody in all His creation.

This punishment teaching is taught in the church. The
preachers say it is the Word of the Bible, and I know well that it
seems to be found in many places in the New Testament. I shall
take an example; Matt 8:12, 22:13, 24:51 and 25:30, where they
speak of the outer darkness, "these men will weep and gnash
their teeth"; Matt 13:42 about "the furnace of fire: there men
will weep and gnash their teeth"; and Matt 25:41 about "the
eternal fire prepared for the devil and his angels", and "in this
place the weeds will burn" (Matt 13:30), "and they (the
ungodly) will go away into eternal punishment." Let this suffice
from the New Testament, but in the Augsburg Confession in
Article 2 it is stated "that original sin judges the guilty and
sends to eternal punishment all those who are not reborn in
baptism and the Holy Spirit"; and in Article 9, it is stated that
they prejudge the rebaptized who reject infant baptism and
assert that the children can be saved without baptism.
However, in Article 17 they prejudge the rebaptized who teach
that there is an end to the punishment meted out to the
condemned and the devils. But what is this? This is not
momentary suffering nor the pains we can lay on one or
another, not human pain that is endured during a human life

time, but eternal pain. Though a person suffer for an entire life time, 80-100 years, this is not much compared to eternity, just like a single drop in the ocean. Yes, what are 100,000 years or a million years of suffering compared to eternal suffering? Think of the age of the celestial universe, a billion or trillion years, one heavenly orb on top of another, one celestial system created from another. But the sinner is no nearer his absolution through all that time passed by him in the torment and the terror of the condemned; and he suffers all that for those years which he has lived here on earth, sometimes in sin, but usually more or less sinless. He suffers unendingly, unlimited torment for limited sin committed during a limited time. But we know that everywhere the consequence follows the cause. We do not know a single instance in the natural system, of the opposite, namely that eternal punishing torments are meted out for a few sins. The age of the universe is measured in billions or trillions of years, but this would be as a few seconds in the torment of the sinner.

How should we now believe? Whether hope or God's love and compassion or repentance could light up this despairing night? The souls must have looked forward in this darkness enraged and desperate; yes, if it was possible to imagine that God hated all on heaven and earth, then it should be this way. And who goes there* now? All sinners, all unbelievers, all infidels? Yes, the denominations (many sects) say it often about one another, that all go there who have a different set of beliefs. "Sine ecclesia nulla salves", says the Catholic church. (Outside the church no one is saved). Everybody goes there who is not reborn by baptism of the Holy Spirit, says the Augsburg Confession. The roads to it are broad, and many know the way. Very few get through the narrow path, as witness, "Many are called, but few are chosen." Think now of that great multitude. There are only a few in my own denomination** that get by. All the others go to the flaming fire! So think, one and all. All other groups, all other denominations, go into the deep that boils in fire and brimstone. Thus most of the people in Asia, Africa, American, Australia, and Europe go there. In addition, as if that is not sufficient, all those thousands of millions who

* presumably to hell
** at the time, Lutheran

lived on earth before Christ will go there* over the centuries so
many that we do not know their number. The Augburg
Confession clearly condemns all the unbaptized to go there.
The 400 million Budhists will go there, as will the 200 million
Moslems, the nearly 200 million Brahmins, the millions of
dark-skinned people of the southern hemisphere, millions in
other heathen lands. Undoubtedly the majority of people who
will live on earth for untold centuries, most of eternity, will go
there because even if mankind was once perfect, now they will
sink deeper and deeper in sin.

Then it is best not to expect better things than hitherto. And
we look now to the heavens and see the untold numbers of
stars, which are all suns with whole legions of planets, perhaps
with living beings like ourselves. Where should these go except
the broad way like others? There go all the host of fallen angels
who were condemned to Hell, and chained there in darkness, to
be kept there till Judgement Day. We thus see that in the end it
is no small place. But then the torment in this place! Who can
describe it? Human pen cannot begin to describe eternal
torment, for with the experience we now have, we need an ever-
working almighty force to ensure that these pitiful sinners can
continue to suffer. All that we know from scientific evidence is
that the body will burn in fire until it returns to its origins; it
rots in the earth; it withers in age; it wastes away from great
pain. For all this I say, we need an ever-working almighty
power to keep the body suffering, to renew it, and give it new
energy so that it can continue to suffer.

We have often been told in detail about this suffering. People
have gone all out to make the description the most pathetic,
dreadful, and frightening. But as is natural, people have come
near it. People have roasted others in ovens, baked them on
pans, boiled them in oil as did the Inquisition, skinned them
alive as did the Turks, sawed them in half from end to end as
did David or Ivan the Terrible, burned them in a fire at the
stake as did the Inquisition and the Church Councils, buried
them alive, torn them limb from limb between wild horses,
nailed them to the cross as did the Romans, cut them up piece
by piece, tarred them, pierced them with a sword, and lit them
like candles as did Nero. But none of this can compare with

* to hell

eternal, everlasting torment that never ceases. What incomparable horror, what fright it would be, would it not, if any of this were true? What a spiteful God such a God must be who lays such suffering on beings created in His own image, who thus tortures parts of Himself! What are the cruellest hangmen of humanity, what are Caligula, Nero, and Ivan the Terrible compared to Him? They had a momentary pleasure to witness the torment, but this God, who is responsible for condeming some people, looks on it with pleasure from eternity to eternity!

But some want to add and say, in contradiction to Biblical teaching about the resurrection of the body, that it is the soul that is tormented by everlasting pangs of conscience. But when one gives this consideration, it appears all the worse, for what are the pains of the body compared to the pains of the soul? Whoever has had feelings of guilt for a broken deed, whoever has experienced prolonged sorrow or a broken heart, whoever has uncontrolled passion break up his strength, whoever has experienced the great separation at the loss of a loved one, whoever has tried to give his beloved unavailable hope, he has an idea bout it. Doesn't sorrow sometimes affect people in such a way, that they become insane or drop down dead? Do not the pangs of guilt affect many in such a way that they have neither happiness nor peace? One wishes for nothing but death when the accusations overcome him so that he curses his own birth; and instead of enduring these pains, he gives up. Even though he would believe in eternal wisdom, he gives up, I say, going to this place* by taking his own life. No! This explanation, that hell is an eternal guilt trip, does nothing to solve the problem; on the other hand, it makes it even more distant and unsolvable.

From all these innumerable souls that are to suffer and be tormented in the eternal fire, a cry of distress and a scream of pain are raised up before the throne of the heavenly king. Sometimes it has been said that the chosen enjoy the pains of the damned; moreover, that their scream of pain were but one part of an anthem of praise that sounds through the heavens, and rings sweetly in the ears of the Almighty. But what terror, what folly to utter such things! How can God be the

*Presumably, to hell.

ETERNAL LOVE, how can He be the ALL-WISE; how can
He be the ALMIGHTY? Is any power so great that it, can
oppose Him? Must God tolerate His enemy as He does His
friend, and submit to the Devil? But presumably if souls which
are created in God's image, depart from His way, they must be
eternally damned. Does the Devil, in warring against the
Almighty, still leave the victory in doubt? Or has God, who has
created everything — angels, spirits, all beings — has He
created the dominion for his enemies, yes in reality a large and
powerful dominion? But He has Himself, whereas the majority
of nations and religious sects should listen to the angels of the
evil one; for narrow is the way that leads to Life and few find
their way. Almighty God is then in a corner of the Heavens and
has had to sell a portion of His realm and subjects into the
hands of his enemy. And all these beings, angels, spirts, and
mankind, God created in the beginning, knowing beforehand,
how all would progress, how the angels would fall, how men
would disobey, how these, His handiwork and His images,
would end up in the predetermined fire of torture. How awfully
He went wrong! How He misjudged when He surveyed all He
created and saw it was hardly good! Or where is His love, His
eternal, immeasurable, all-embracing compassion? Compare
His compassion with the compassion of persons, those
ordinary and imperfect beings. Does a father not forgive his
child if it has disobeyed? Does he not try over and over again,
in every way, to lead it to righteousness? If that fails, then it is
not because the father does not want it to materialize, but
rather because he does not have the power to bring it about.
How is the mother's love for her child manifested? She
embraces it with her love; she prays for it if it walks the wrong
path; she spreads her arms to greet the lost but later found son;
she does not hesitate to lay down her own life if need be to set
her child free. And how often do people not forgive their
enemies? Would you not suppose, dear friends, that God is
equally just, compassionate, and merciful as men? But now we
know that He has the will to save all, and we also know that He
has the might and means to make His will known. How can it
then be that most of the universe ends up in eternal damnation?
What an absurdity it is to consider God so incomplete,
vengeful, and ignorant that He should condemn Himself, when

it is acknowledged that all mankind, each and every person, is created in His image, whether a Greek or a Jew, Chinese or Black, Tartar or Indian where all acknowledge that all these are His children!

Men say that this *is what Jesus Christ taught, but I do not believe it. He has never expressed it at least in that sense which the church most often proclaims. Those alleged instances in which He proclaims eternal damnation appear to be based on misunderstanding, distortion, or false information such as the text today (for this sermon) wherein Christ is to have said, "Go from me, you cursed, into that eternal fire, prepared for the devil and his angels." We know well that Christ did not, himself, write a single word of what is found in the New Testament. He did not expect his disciples to write a single word; no gospel was written until at least 30 - 40 years after the crucifixion of Christ. It was clerics and monks who much later decided what manuscript should be considered authentic, and rejected as unauthentic a large quantity of gospels, record books, revelations and letters.

We also know that theologians have been embroiled in a great controversy about the words "eternal" and "eternity" where some would relate them to endless time, but others a specified time.

That Christ could never have been able to teach eternal punishment, every one must admit, who believes or accepts the love of the Heavenly Father and the love of Jesus Christ. It seems to me to be impossible to believe otherwise. Where do we see such hatred in the life of Jesus Christ? Christ healed the sick, raised the dead to life, gave sight to the blind, bread to the hungry, consolation to the bereaved, strength to the sick, and hope to the downtrodden. He says Himself, "Come to me all who labor and are heavy laden and I will give you rest." He says "ALL" excepts no one, no nation, no sect, no sinner. He even says that He has not come to lead the righteous to God, but sinners.

What should we think about the teaching which condemns infants if they die before baptism, and makes it absolute as in the case of the Augsburg Confession (Arts. 24 and 9) that they go to the eternal fire? What is their sin? Where is the justice of

*eternal damnation

the heavenly and the eternal that we know is higher, cleaner, and more sublime, than all human righteousness? I can hardly think of anyone who has such an enemy, that he would want him punished for eternity. Men take their revenge, men kill others, men torture others, but if it were proposed to condemn men to eternal torment, then most men would hesitate; I suppose that the most brutish and savage tyrants would hesitate. Or could anyone who reads this imagine that he has such an enemy that he would wish him unrelenting pain? I suppose no such person exists. But infants judging by some teachings, should be scourged by a judgment of a righteous God. What a concept of God! I am certain that every uncorrupted person who thinks about it, must shudder at the enormity that, with these teachings, is put upon the Creator's shoulders. But it has been put there, and still is today, by those who, for example, accept the Augsburg Confession which states that no one can be saved who is not baptized. All unbaptized nations, all unbaptized children, are naturally citizens of the Devil from this point of view. This does not seem to be well ordered to kindle love from Him whom we should love with all the might of our souls and body. It is as if people wish to get everything into an open fire of hatred with the Heavenly Father, that people would want to kill all belief in Him and all hope and longing of the heart after being in contact with Him. I cannot believe this; this has been invented at a time of revenge and cruelty, when human life was regarded as worthless, before men had fully prepared to cast off their brutish ways and before the concept of love had taken root among nations. Perhaps one could thereby hold nations in fear and dread — hold them down, so that they dared not raise their heads high. That this has been fulfilled in those early days we can see from numerous examples of history. We can see still today that many people become phrenetic mostly because of this teaching; that many die in despair about the salvation of their souls.

I also doubt that this is the teaching of the Bible, for Paul the Apostle speaks about the time when God shall be "all in everything" (I Cor 15,28). He says that everything shall be under one domain in Christ, both that which is in heaven and on earth (Eph 1, 10), and as all die in Christ, will all live in

Christ; and likewise this, that all shall bow before Him both in Heaven and on Earth; and this, that all tongues shall acknowledge Him to be the Lord. Here it is evident that one must reinterpret all these quotes if one is to find damnation, because they contradict this view. Nevertheless then, it is impossible for me to believe in such damnation, and I want to measure the truth of each Article of faith with that, to determine whether it recognized Hell or not. Whoever promotes it, I'd say, is not promoting God's truth. It is so contrary to the Creator's nature; it is so opposite to all that is the most truthful, natural and righteous as we know it; it sets the Creator's nature lower than man's. I must either reject this doctrine or reject God; but God be praised, I have no doubts about this.

The source of evil will be no clearer although men make themselves a devil, and endow him with sense. God must have created him as he did all beings. And then it come to light that God is All-Present; in all His realm, nowhere is there a vacant spot in the universe, where God is not present, working with his power. Will anyone say that God of the Heavens will 'fulfill' the place of torture of the damned with His nearness? It seems unlikely to me. But it becomes clear, if men watch, that the struggle between the flesh and the spirit is the struggle between the bodily sins and the sinless, spiritual, and eternal aspect of the divine nature of mankind.

Man has never been as perfect as now; he has always been stumbling from the time he first walked the earth; he has steadily been pushing forward toward greater fulfulment, according to the plan of the allwise Creator. Although man has not progressed far, yet God be praised for man's many victories. With His help, in the end we will reach the goal which He has intended for us. With this viewpoint men have no need for punishment or damnation, because it would be impossible to make these a part of the Lord's plan. As for the contact between those who have gone to eternal bliss and those who go to eternal punishment, how have you viewed it? It is our belief and holy conviction that God has given us love in our hearts to palliate life's struggles, to bind us, one with another, to be able to experience the most blessed times in this world, when friend loves friend, when men love their Creator and Lord. Think now about when death comes and separates friend from friend, child from mother, son from father. The father, mother, friend then go to heaven and do not find there those whom they loved most of all in this life, but know of them in the tortures of Hell. Can we imagine that they would enjoy the bliss of heaven? Or that the love of friend and child would be completely cast out? Has our heavenly Father worked for nought in all that He gave — Love? Has He made nothing of His love offerings?

Most of us imagine, that in another life we would see our elderly parents and friends who have left us. But wait! If the teaching of damnation is true, then many in heaven can expect to miss their beloved mother, father, or friend. Or then, you parents, would you expect to see all your children? No, definitely no! If the teaching of damnation true, then you could expect the majority of those friends to be in the nether world, because there are few who know the narrow path. But do you imagine that you would be happy — blessed — knowing that your beloved children are in eternal torture? Would the bliss be blemished? However, this punishment cannot exist, because the best, the holiest, purest, most divine emotion in your hearts — love — cries out an ETERNAL NO! I am convinced that none of us are so inclined that we could be callous about the cries of pain and distress raised by loved ones; that we would shut our eyes to heaven, if we saw flesh of our flesh and blood of our blood in a bubbling fiery pool. None of us could believe in a God who, having created mankind in His own image, would then with-hold God's love from man and impose on him instead the dread and revenge of God from which mankind would naturally shrink with fear and trembling. If it were as some believe now, that this trembling were justified, what do we think we can do about it, if we look over our children, knowing that most of them will end up in eternal damnation? It would be a major sin to bear them into this world, blessed children; it would be the moral duty of each and every one of us to make a determined effort to eliminate mankind from the earth. Better that no one be born, than a few endure eternal torture! What then about this multitude? Better that the whole world be destroyed than a single person go to the eternal fire!

But there is no danger in this, bcause there is so much evidence against eternal punishment: especially God's own nature, His omniscience, His righteousness, His almightiness and His love. We see that the One who is infinitely good must desire the welfare of His own child, the All-wise must know how to bring it about and the Almighty must be able to sustain it. Who can imagine that God the Father had created the world and then, having done so, could not control His own creation? Or is it divine justice to punish people with **eternal** damnation for sins that are committed over a relatively short period of 20, 30, 60, or even 70 years? The punishment would be endless much greater than the crime. How can we imagine this about our loving Father? If we think of all the good He grants us, all the blessings that He lets come our way, and if we would accept them, then in our hearts we mut realize how wrong it is for us to endow Him with such ruthlessness. We must let our doubts about this light up in our hearts. Then love and trust of Him will be rekindled as He embraces us in His love from cradle to grave. To Him we must give thanks for all the good and true and beautiful, both in us and in nature around us. We must give thanks to Him who has given us life, love, faith, and hope; to Him who we know and believe will never let His eyes or hands off his children; to Him who gave us part of His divinity, so that we are able to be united with Him.

But I certainly do not want to assuage or diminish punishment for committed sins. For as I am convinced that our loving heavenly Father has never intended anyone to be tortured in eternal damnatioon, so am I convinced that He must punish us for even the smallest transgression. But the punishment is to be related to our betterment, for in that way we improve more and more; we come closer and closer to the light of our eternal, beneficent Father. Punishment is one of the Lord's plans in this world to lead souls to Himself, to peace, and to bliss.

Oh, thou God and Father of our hearts, let us thy children learn to love Thee, worship and adore Thee as the eternal source of love. Rid us of all demeaning thoughts, rid us of all which keeps us from knowing Thee as Thou art, almighty, holy, good, and wise. Let us obey Thy commands, as Thy truly loving children, trying ever to come nearer to Thee, nearer and nearer to the light of truth and justice. Oh Thou who embraces the universe with Thy grace, Thou who fulfills all reality with thy nearness, be Thou our Lord and enlighten our spirits about the true and just and make us acceptable to Thee. Be Thou our God and Father in life and death in Jesus' name.

Ed. Note: In the editing of the literal translation of this sermon from Icelandic to English, it has been necessary to repunctuate it in some places and to alter the wording in others. This has been accomplished without altering the intended meaning.

GEB

Appendix E

The Founders of
The New Iceland Conference

CONSTITUTION/BYLAWS — BREIÐUVÍK (BROAD BAY) CONGREGATION

1. The congregation confesses as a foundation for its beliefs, God the father, son and spirit; the father creator and sustainer of the Universe; the son savior of humanity, fulfillment of deity, and image of His being; the spirit the working of God's power in the Universe.

2. The congregation places the Bible as the foundation of its faith, and accepts God's revelation of it, in spirit but not literally.

3. The congregation does not bind itself to any contracts or agreements of former synods or Christian church conferences as being absolute. The eternal everlasting damnation it completely rejects.

4. The purpose of the congregation is to promote and to strengthen liberal faith and Christian love, both among their own members, and wherever it has influence.

5. Our church practices shall be the same as before such as worship, christening, confirmation, communion, marriages, funerals and [sic] etc.

6. The congregation belongs to the Icelandic Church conference in this country, and its Articles of Union are binding.

7. The trustees of the congregations are authorized to accept into membership whoever desires if he accepts these articles.

8. The annual meeting shall be held annually in the month of June; where trustees shall be elected, the finances of the past year approved, budget for the forthcoming year set forth, and other necessary business taken up.

A second congregational meeting shall be held annually in November to determine the minister's expenses, necessary congregational expenses, etc.

9. In addition, special congregational meetings can be called, by the Minister or the Trustees, or when requested by five voting members in writing stating the purpose of the meeting.

10. No meeting shall be called with less than seven days' notice and a written call. Every call shall specify the main agenda item to be considered.

11. Congregational meetings have the power to adjudicate and direct all congregational business; only a majority vote is necessary.

12. Should a congregational meeting be held in the absence of the president, one of the other trustees will call the meeting, and the meeting shall have a moderator. If a trustee moves or dies, another shall be elected, if need arises.

13. Officers of the congregation are: the pastor, three trustees, two auditors, and one alternate trustee; the trustees shall elect a president, secretary and treasurer from their number. Trustees and auditors are elected only for one year. All these officers shall be responsible for the welfare of the congregation.

14. The congregation shall authorize its delegates to negotiate for a pastor annually at the annual meeting of the conference in March. The pastor has the same duties as pastors do in Lutheran churches.

15. The pastor can resign with 3 months notice, and the same is also true if the congregation wishes to dismiss the pastor.

16. The trustees are responsible for the executive power of the congregation. The president shall appoint committees, call meetings and preside at them; the secretary shall conduct the correspondence of the congregation; the treasurer shall be in charge of the congregation's income — he shall make payments with the consent of the trustees or the congregation. An accounting of income and expenditures for the preceeding year shall be given by the treasurer at the annual meeting, together with a report from the auditors.

17. The congregation as a whole, and each member, is obliged to work for the Christian nurture and teaching of those children who are in the congregation, and shall therefore conduct a Sunday School as long as there is a need.

18. Both because of the law of the land and because of public morals and decency, every member shall avoid unnecessary labor on Sundays and Holidays.

19. The congregation obligates itself to compensate the minister on regular days, the annual salary that he has been promised. Each member who has voting rights must contribute to the congregation's needs in rightful proportion to the abilities of others.

20. Those members who are 15 years of age have voting and election rights, but 18 year old members have eligibility if they have paid their pledge for the congregation's needs that are then due.

21. The fiscal year of the congregation is from July 1 to June 30.

22. Trustees may rent the meeting house to travelling clergy, missionaries, lecturers, or others for worship services or for lectures, if they consider that the majority of the congregation agrees.

23. All voting members who are at home should attend every congregational meeting.

24. Should someone disobey the congregation's 'laws' or work against the congregation, or dishonor it with his conduct, this is grounds for dismissal, should he not respond to friendly reminders, and the congregation unanimously finds him guilty.

25. Should someone desire to resign his membership, then he should give notification at a congregational meeting or notify by letter to the pastor or the trustees, and give his reasons. Whoever resigns at the same time forfeits all rights as a member and claims to his property, but he is bound to contribute all that he has pledged.

26. These by-laws will not be amended except with a two-thirds vote; the amendment must have been brought up and discussed at the previous congregational meeting.

The above by-laws are signed by:

Magnús J. Skaptason	*Gunnar I. Helgason*
I. Hildibrandsson	*Sigurður J. Vídal*
Jón Bjarnason	*Baldwin Jónsson*
Jóhannes Jónasson	*Sigurgeir Einarsson*
Jón Jónsson	*Jón Sigurðsson*
John B. Snæfeld	*Lárus Guðjónsson*
Kv. B. Snæfeld	*Einar Th. Dalman*
Finnbogi Finnbogasson	*Guðríður Th. Dalman*

Bjarni E. Dalmann
Jón Frímann Kristjánsson
Kristín Jónsdóttir
Sigurður Guðmundsson
Ingveldur Jósephsdóttir
Jóhanna Steinvör
    Sigurðardóttir
Grímur Grímsson
Sigurrós S. Vídal
Sigurlaug S. Vídal
   (Mrs. E.J. Montgomery)
Jónas Jónsson
Eggert Jónasson
Einar Markússson
Ingibjörg Guðmundardóttir
Arnfriður Jónsdóttir

Helga L. Guðmundsdóttir
Sigurrós Markusdottir
Björg Markúsdóttir
Ása Einarsdottir
Agnes Jónatansdóttir
Benedikta M. Helgadóttir
Kristín Grímsdóttir
Arnfriður Jansdóttir
Gudbjörg Bjarnadóttir
Þorunn Jónsdóttir
Sigmundur Gunnarsson
Jónina G. Jansdóttir
Sigrún Sigmundsdóttir
Mrs. J. Nordal
Guðmundur Markúson
Jón Guðmundsson

Supporters of Magnus Skaptason, Spring 1893, as per letters to Heimskringla

GIMLI

Gottskálk Sigfússon
Jón Guðmundson
Jóhann P. Solmundsson
Kr. Lifmann
Magnús Halldórsson
Albert Kristjánsson
Björn Jónsson
Thorarinn Thorleifsson
Baldvin Andersson
Lárus Guðjónsson
Guðjón Lárusson
Joseph Sigurðsson
Thorsteinn Sigfússon
Gudl. Magnússon
G.M. Thompson
Th. J. Jonssen

Ólafur Sigurðsson
Rögnvaldur Jónsson
Hannes Thorvaldsson
Sigurður Th. Kristjánsson
Magnús Guðlaugsson
Jakob Oddsson
Sigurður Jakobsson
Karvel Halldórsson
Friðfinnur Einarsson
Jóhann Stefánsson
Jóhannes Ólafsson
Jónas Ingimar Schaldemose
Jónas Skúlason
G. Guðmundsson
B. Jónsson
Th. Guðmundsson

Kristan S. Guðmundsson
John Dalstead
John Stevens
Jón Rögnvaldsson
Asm. Thorsteinsson
Peter Guðlaugsson
Jón Stefánsson
Gestur Oddleifsson
Hannes Hannesson
Jakob Sigurgeirsson
Kristján Guðmundsson
J. Guðmundsson
Vigfús Thorsteinsson
Oddur Árnason
Daníel Daníelsson
Jakob Guðmundson
Halldór Karvelsson
Guðmundur Ólafsson
Halldór Brynjólfsson
Gísli Sveinsson
Joseph Freeman
Chris Paulsson
Magnús F. Thorláksson
Hans Jonsson
Ásmundur Einarsson

Jóhannes Hannesson
Th. Paulson
H.G. Thiðriksson
J.A. Hanneson
Jón Sigurðsson
Johann Jonsson
Jón Jóhannson
Valdimar Thorsteinsson
Bjarni Pálmason
Guðmundur Bjarnason
Jónas Jóhannesson
Jóhann P. Árnason
Árni Oddson
Sigurður Einarsson
Hafliði Guðmundsson
Páll Gunnlaugsson
Thorvaldur Sveinsson
Kristján Kjernested
Vigfús Benediksson
Jóhann H. Schaldemose
G.R. Baldwin
Jónas Bergmann
Sveinn Rúnolfsson
St. Ó Eiríksson

ARNES

Sigurður Sigurbjörnsson
Jónas Jónsson
Gísli Jónsson
Jón Jónsson
Jonas Magnusson

Einar Guðmundsson
Hjörleifur Björnsson
G. Hannesson
Gunnar Gíslason

Appendix F

Magnús J. Skaptason
Memorial Celebration

‚Ѵ//////////////////////////////////Ъ

CELEBRATION OF THE NINETIETH ANNIVERSARY OF REV MAGNÚS SKAFTASON'S CONVERSION TO UNITARIAN-UNIVERSALISM

The obituaries re-printed below appeared in two Winnipeg newspapers in March, 1932. They record the highlights of Rev. Magnús Skaptason's career in the Unitarian ministry which began circa 1890:

Rev. Magnús J. Skaptason, one of the first Icelandic Unitarian ministers in western Canada, died at the home of his daughter, Mrs. M.B. Halldórson, wife of Dr. M.B. Halldórson, in Winnipeg, Man., March 8, at the age of eighty-two.

The funeral service was held at the Federated Church and was conducted by Dr. Rögnvaldur Pétursson and Rev. Benjamin Kristjánsson, minister of the church. It was preceded by a short service at the home of Dr. Halldórson, conducted by Rev. Philip M. Pétursson of the Unitarian church of Winnipeg.

Mr. Skaptason was born in Iceland, February 4, 1850. He was a graduate of the Reykjavík College and Divinity School. He was ordained in 1875, and served for twelve years as minister in the State Church of Iceland. In 1887, accompanied by his wife and children, he came to Manitoba where he carried on a successful ministry in the Gimli district for a number of years.

Early in his ministry here he experienced difficulty in subscribing to the doctrines of the Lutheran Synod, and he withdrew from it, being followed by the churches to which he had been ministering.

Soon after that he became minister of the First Icelandic Unitarian Church in Winnipeg, succeeding Rev. Björn Pétursson its founder. In 1901 he was one of the chief organizers and first president of the Icelandic Unitarian Conference.

During the years that followed he traveled among the Icelandic communities in Manitoba and Saskatchewan, preaching the gospel of sweet reasonableness and freedom of mind. He was well liked everywhere for his sincerity and independence of thought, and he gained a large and loyal following.

He spent a few years in the settlements in Minnesota and North Dakota, as well as on the West Coast, and returned to Winnipeg in 1912, where he has since resided at the home of his daughter.

During his ministry in the Gimli district he became engaged in the publication of the religious periodical **Dagsbrún**, and while in Winnipeg he edited and published the journal **Fróði**. In 1913 he became editor of the Icelandic paper, **Heimskringla**, and continued in that position until 1917, when he retired from active work at the age of sixty-seven. After that, however, acceding to the requests to speak on special occasions, he continued for a few years to pay occasional visits to the Icelandic communities.

To the very end he maintained a vital interest in the progress of the communities and churches in which he played an early and prominent part. He was held in high esteem always, and is mourned by all who knew him.

The large number of people in attendance at the funeral service and the many messages of sympathy from outside points, bore tribute to the respect in which this pioneer of religious liberty was held among the Icelanders in western Canada.

As long as Icelanders and the organizations they have built up in America continue to exist, his name will be remembered for his honesty, sincerity, and independence of thought.

He is survived by three daughters, Mrs. M.B. Halldórson, Mrs. W. Cook of Winnipeg, and Mrs. W.H. Adams of Bottineau, N.D. and by one son, Joseph Skaptason of Chicago, Ill.

P.M.P.

Rev. Magnús J. Skaptason, one of the first Icelandic ministers in western Canada, died at the home of his daughter, Mrs. M.B. Halldórson in Winnipeg, Manitoba, on March 8, 1932 at the age of eighty-two. Mr. Skaptason was born in Iceland, February 4, 1850. He was a graduate of the Reykjavik College and Divinity School. He was ordained in 1875, and served for twelve years as minister in the State Church of Iceland. In 1887, accompanied by his wife and children, he came to Manitoba, where he carried on a successful ministry in the Gimli district for a number of years. During this time he experienced a change in theological views, and withdrew from the Lutheran Synod, followed by many of the churches to which he had been ministering. He became minister of the First Icelandic Church in Winnipeg. In 1901 he was one of the organizers of the Icelandic Unitarian Conference. To the end of his life he maintained a vital interest in the progress of the Icelandic churches in which he had played a prominent part.

He is survived by three daughters, Mrs. M.B. Halldórson, Mrs. W. Cook of Winnipeg, and Mrs. W.H. Adams of Bottineau, N.D., and by one son, Joseph Skaptason of Chicago, Ill.

In July 1980, Rev. V. Emil Gudmundson initiated plans for a formal public observance of the 90th anniversary of Skaptason's conversion to Unitarianism. He did so by circulating a memo among Unitarians in Winnipeg and the "New Iceland" communities:

A NINETIETH ANNIVERSARY

1891 was a lively year among Icelandic settlers not only in Winnipeg, but fully as much in New Iceland. The Rev. Magnús J. Skaptason who had come from Iceland in 1887 to serve the Lake Winnipeg Lutheran Parish, grew increasingly disenchanted with the doctrine of eternal damnation for all who are unbaptized. New Year's Eve 1890 was the first time he chose to share his views with his congregations. In March 1891 he elaborated his beliefs in a sermon which closely resembles Universalist preaching of the latter part of the nineteenth century, and resigned from the Icelandic Lutheran Synod. He appears to have a majority in sympathy with his views in five of his congregations, although only three clearly withdrew from the Synod, while organizing "The Free Christian Association of Icelandic Lutherans in America." The original by-laws of this group of congregations deleted only the reference to eternal damnation and the divine revelation of the Bible. Later these congregations became the nucleus for the Unitarian Churches of New Iceland and later still the Federated Churches.

In 1980, the author wrote:

"I propose that a fitting observance be held in the summer of 1981 which might include the following:"

- A special service in which the 1891 sermon of Skaptason is preached in translation (I have translated it but it does need editing).
- A dramatic presentation of some of the major events of this early period; again I have quite a number of documents etc. in my possession.

- A photographic display depicting this history.
- A "pilgrimage" to the sites of the congregations in this large parish Mikley, Breiduvik, Gimli, Vidines (the locations of the congregations known i.e. the 1891 sites: Mikley, Bræðra Söfnuður?
- Enactment of the service with period attire, horse drawn vehicles etc.
- Banquet at Hecla Island
- Some visiting at the camp in Hnausa

Arrangements should be made as much as possible here in Manitoba preferably by a committee of volunteers we can gather this summer. To fit my calendar it would have to be either the second weekend in July or the second, third, or fourth weekends in August.

Emil Gudmundson
Minneapolis, July 1980

This was followed up in May, 1981 with another memo from Emil Gudmundson:

UNITARIAN UNIVERSALIST ASSOCIATION
of Churches and Fellowships in North America

V. Emil Gudmundson, D.D.
Interdistrict Representative   May 14, 1981

TO UNITARIAN FRIENDS in/from/interested in
NEW ICELAND
FROM EMIL GUDMUNDSON

ABOUT 90 YEARS OF RELIGIOUS LIBERALISM IN NEW ICELAND:

A recent note from Pálmi Pálsson of Arborg reminds me of our general discussions last summer and in March about doing something to observe this anniversary of the ministry of Magnús Skaptason and others and he informs me that the Arborg Church's annual meeting discussed this matter and are interested in pursuing it with perhaps something at Hecla Island. This winter I asked Kristine Kristofferson about the possibility of using the Gimli church for a service and she assured me this was possible providing ample notice of such a plan is given to the lessee.

I have Sunday, July 19th marked in my calendar, but I could also consider Aug. 16th (isn't that the week after the Arborg fair?) Incidentally I discovered that a 50th anniversary service was held at Gimli forty years ago June 29th, 1941.

What we need is rather fast input to firm up plans and I begin this as a round robin. I suggest that we communicate with Palmi about your preferences and ideas and I'll keep in touch with him. I think one of the needs is to make (the affair) as simple and as attractive and available to everyone interested as possible, and so with this in mind I offer this suggested plan as a starter:

1. A church service at Gimli on Sun. July 19th (Aug. 16 as an alternative) at 11 a.m.
2. Have lunch at the Hnausa Camp at 1 p.m: Potluck picnic or whatever people like Palmi, Vordís, Alice, Lauga, Solla and others at Arborg think best.
3. Late in the afternoon, like 4:30 p.m., make a pilgrimage to the sites of Magnús Skaptason's early ministry such as Hnausa, Hecla etc.
4. Have dinner at Gull Harbor for those that wish at 7 p.m. or so.
5. Vesper service at the Hecla Church or some other appropriate site.

On July 19, 1981, the anniversary celebration began in the Gimli Unitarian Church (then leased to another religious group) with the announcement which follows:

WELCOME! to this service commemorating the Ninetieth anniversary of the introduction of Liberal Religion to New Iceland by the Reverend Magnús J. Skaptason. A great many people have had a hand in making this observance and service a reality and are owed a great deal of appreciation.

Please note that there are activities scheduled for the remainder of the day, and everyone is invited to join us for those.

Immediately following the service everyone is invited to join in caravan style to drive north to Arnes for a stop at the Vilhjálmur Stefánsson Memorial to pay tribute briefly to perhaps the most famous of Icelandic Unitarians and one-time student at the Harvard Divinity School.

The caravan will continue to the Unitarian Camp at Hnausa where a catered lunch smorgasbord will be served at 1 p.m. at the cost of $5.00.

The afternoon will be informal with the possibilities of swimming or other activities. There will be a time for the sharing of both mementos and memories and perhaps singing. Later, significant sights at Hnausa will be visited such as the Skaptason home site and the site of the first church.

About 6 p.m. there will be a brief vesper service by the Mikley Church on Hecla Island. Some persons are planning to have dinner at the Gull Harbor Lodge at 7 p.m.

For information speak to Mr. Gudmundson, Pálmi Pálsson, Margaret and Eric Bjornson, Stefanía Sigurðsson, or Kristine Kristofferson or anyone else wearing a yellow ribbon.

Following this announcement, Rev. V. Emil Gudmundson delivered a sermon wherein he paid tribute to Rev. Magnús Skaptason and quoted appropriate passages from his "Breakaway" sermon (See Appendix D).

At the conclusion of the service the congregation formed a caravan which proceeded to the site of a cairn which had been erected in memory of the late Dr. Vilhjálmur Stefánsson near his birthplace at Arnes, Manitoba. This pilgramage was included in the itinerary because Stefánsson, a fellow Unitarian, had been a contemporary of Skaptason; also because he was held in high regard by the Icelandic community in general because of his eminence as an Arctic explorer and writer.

From Arnes the group travelled to the Unitarian Camp at Hnausa, Manitoba for a noon-hour luncheon. The early afternoon was spent reminiscing and examining various records and memorabilia which were on display in the chapel on the campsite. Towards evening a pilgrimage was made to Rev. Magnús Skaptason's former home at Hnausa, Manitoba.

The next stop was made on Hecla Island at the church building erected on the site of the original church where Skaptason had served in his time. Because Hecla Island, including its village, has recently been designated a provincial park, its affairs are now administered by the Manitoba government. The authority in charge had permitted the use of the church building for a brief vesper service as requested, but cautioned that the **observance must be limited to that**. In his remarks, Emil Gudmundson paid tribute to the pioneers of the church and community. Following the brief stop at the church, the entourage assembled for dinner at the Gull Harbor Hotel on Hecla Island to conclude the day's activities. Special guests representing the clergy were:

Rev. Philip M. Petursson, D.D. - Minister Emeritus, Winnipeg Unitarian Universalist Church; Rev. John Gilbert, Minister, Winnipeg Unitarian Univerasalist-Church; Charlotte Cowtan-Holm and Jane Bramadat, at the time chaplains of the Winnipeg Unitarian Universalist Church.

Members of Rev. Magnús Skaptason's family who attended the celebration included Eleanor Cook, Ralph Cook, and Fred Cook who are his grandchildren, and Kathryn Baranovsky, a great-grandaughter.

G.E.B.

Appendix G

I Was Born A Prairie Unitarian

By V. Emil Gudmundson
Interdistrict Representative
Unitarian Universalist Association
Delivered at Western District CUC
Annual Meeting, September, 1975

I am a third generation Unitarian, although I bear neither a New England heritage nor an "Anglo" name. This, I believe, qualifies me as a minority among minorities (I hope not a freak). Only about 12% of us are "born into the UU faith," according to the 1967 Goals Survey, 1 and I am certain that my category of a born Prairie Ethnic Unitarian would be infinitesimal.

But as a young man growing up on the prairies of Manitoba, it did not occur to me that it was such an odd phenomenon. As I discovered in my late teens, I did not fully understand or appreciate the Unitarianism of my childhood. It was there. After all there were eight congregations (with church buildings) in Manitoba and Saskatchewan — and they formed the "United Conference of Icelandic Churches of North America". Our little congregation at Lundar had a minister, Guðmundur Arnason, who was a very good family friend as well as minister — and was a graduate of the Meadville Theological School. I met or knew slightly several other ministers who served the other churches. In addition to these congregations, there were as many as ten preaching stations where services were held occasionally; some of these circuits were served by our minister.

As I try to put together the associations that I have with our local church and with Unitarianism during my childhood and youth (1930-45), I find them disjointed, and the wonder may be that I did not become a drop-out as most of my contemporaries from that community did.

In the first place there was no regular Sunday School. Most of the church membership (maybe 60) were farmers spread over a 10-mile radius of town. But there was a small concentration in our immediate area, and so for two summers we did have Sunday School in our local one-room schoolhouse. I have two recollections: first, the stories in **Heroic Lives** 2, and second, is that we learned to read Icelandic, and one story we heard was "Nail Soup" a variation of "Stone Soup".

Secondly, I believe services were held monthly, and all services and sermons were in the Icelandic language, since it was the language of the older generation, such as my grandparents. This meant, however, that my generation had little interest. However, there was one type of service I do remember — and that is confirmation. The confirmands (ages 14 and 15) attended classes for about six months of Saturdays with the minister, and even this service was mostly in Icelandic. Somehow, I "fell between the cracks" and was missed, but this appeared to be a big event — I still got my new suit of clothes.

One of the Icelandic-language weeklies, **Heimskringla,** published in Winnipeg was Unitarian in religious sentiment and conservative in its political leaning.Since I read this paper and discussed it with my grandparents, I knew about the Unitarian ministers of the prairies (as many as five active at a time). I later discovered some never had Unitarian ministerial fellowship. I knew about Boston and Meadville and Thomas Jefferson and Regional Directors, and the Annual Conference (Kirkjuthing). Perhaps this was the necessary imprinting.

Our local minister and his wife were personal friends of my grandparents and parents. In pioneer fashion — during the depression — a variety of produce from the farm was given to them. I am not aware that much money was ever contributed to the church.

The heartbeat of the congregation was the Ladies' Aid "Eining" (means Unity). Both my mother and grandmother were members, and my mother was especially active. In addition to support of the church, I recall two projects that became traditions and one was definitely for the benefit of persons regardless of race, color, or creed. One was an annual gathering of the older Icelandic citizens of the community, for entertainment, a speaker, conversation, and special foods. The other was the Christmas boxes for the poor, many of whom were Metis.

And lastly one of my earliest recollections is of the church building being high on stilts, while a basement was dug, with horses, and by hand. It seems that my grandfather had a big hand in this venture, and everyone hoped that the stilts would hold. In any event, one of my grandmother's Lutheran neighbors visited her at that time, and told her of a dream she had had. It was that Satan was behind this project, and that the Unitarians would be punished by the building falling in the hole. So, if my grandfather was really a good Christian, he would no longer persist in building that church basement. Fortunately her dream did not materialize.

These are my early associations as a Prairie Unitarian. But this is not sufficient in itself to really account for my religious roots and identity. And so I have sought to go further and deeper than personal remembrances. I believe that an argument can be made that in no way could Unitarianism of the latter part of the 19th century help but become an influence among the Icelandic settlers in Canada and the United States.

The beginnings of Unitarianism in my paternal family occurred long before I was a twinkle in anybody's eye. About the turn of the century the first teacher at my grandparents' country school was a young University of Manitoba student heading for Harvard Divinity School, Thorvaldur Thorvaldsson. He was a Unitarian from Arnes, the community where Vilhjalmur Stefansson was born. Undoubtedly Thorvaldsson and Stefansson were acquainted, for Stefansson was also at Harvard. Unfortunately, while at Harvard, Thorvaldsson died from appendicitis.

Thorvaldsson's influence on this farming community was very great, and several families embraced Unitarianism. His brother, Thorbergur, followed him as a teacher in subsequent years and the die was cast (Thorbergur Thorvaldsson became a renowned researcher and teacher, and a building is named in his honor at the University of Saskatchewan). A congregation was organized in 1907, at Mary Hill, and served by occasional visits from ministers. Shortly thereafter, the congregation bought the little schoolhouse which had been outgrown, and moved it. In 1910 they hosted the 5th conference of the Unitarian Conference of Icelandic churches. One tale I recall from my grandparents is that new chairs were bought and a final coat of varnish applied. But in the summer heat, all the delegates were stuck to their seats.

There is no doubt that it was my paternal grandmother who had the greatest Unitarian influence on me, and this is perhaps best stated by her one-time minister, Rev. Albert Kristjánsson:

> No one (Icelandic Unitarian) was more staunch and steady than your grandmother, Mekkin. Her unswerving dedication to the service of whatever she believed to be true and right and the sacrificial devotion to those she loved or accepted into her circle of friends very soon gave her a special place in the inner circle of our friends. [3]

But the Unitarian beginning among the Icelanders was even earlier than this in Winnipeg and "New Iceland". Actually there are three sources of religious liberalism that were present in the late 19th century among these pioneers. Although these sources seem to be somewhat ideologically different and geographically separate, there is also evidence that there is overlapping.

The first is free thought. The most influential American free thought writer of this time was Robert Ingersoll, and he was translated and read. In the late 1880's some farmers in Pembina County, North Dakota, organized an Ethical Culture Society, and presumably had contact with Felix Adler. The foremost of these farmers was Stephan G. Stephanson, who later moved to Alberta, and became renowned as an Icelandic poet. Another was Björn Pétursson whom we find later in another context.

The second influence was American Unitarianism, by way of the Norwegian Unitarian minister in Minneapolis, Kristofer Janson. It was the same Björn Pétursson mentioned above who emerged as a leader. According to Janson's biographer, Nina Draxten, Pétursson had translated several of Janson's sermons into Icelandic and published them as early as 1887. Janson succeeded in securing Pétursson's financial help for minissionary work among his countrymen. [4]

Pétursson visited Janson and at that time met his second wife to be, Jennie Elizabeth McCaine, a charter member of Unity Unitarian Church in St. Paul. [5] He was instrumental in organizing the Icelandic Unitarian Church in Winnipeg in 1891, and became its minister.

The third influence came from Iceland and manifested itself negatively as dissent within the Lutheran churches, primarily in the Lake Winnipeg area, called "New Iceland". The leader was the Rev. Magnús Skaptason, pastor of a circuit of five congregations. The Rev. Albert Kristjánsson comments on this break:

> Magnús Skaptason confirmed me in 1891, and that same year he broke away from the Lutheran church. He preached an Easter sermon in 1891, beginning at the north end of this line of churches. When he reached Gimli (the southernmost church) bedlam had broken loose and the church had been padlocked against him. In this sermon he denied the doctrine of hell and eternal punishment and other kindred beliefs. And the battle was on.[6]

And so the Free Church of Gimli was organized, for Skaptason was not at first willing to give up his claim as a Lutheran, maintaining that the Synod authorities were in error.

I recall an apocryphal story about Skaptason, that he had the unusual habit of using pepper in his coffee. It seems that several of his most devoted parishioners copied their beloved minister in this eccentricity. When the parson broke from the synod and embraced Unitarianism, his congregation was divided. The lines were finally drawn between the pepper and the non-pepper drinkers. The "peppered" parishioners organized the Free Church with their peppered parson as minister.[7]

But as Albert Kristjansson said:

> We need to be reminded that he has other and more meaningful claims to be remembered with gratitude and honor.

> It would not be altogether inappropriate to say that Björn Pétursson and Magnús J. Skaptason were, for the Unitarian movement among the Icelandic

people in Canada, what Channing and Parker were
for the beginnings of Unitarianism in New England.
And in that equation Parker would be represented
by Skaptasson. 8

During the 1890's, the two congregations at Gimli and
Winnipeg held their own. Björn Pétursson died in 1893, shortly
after a building was erected, and the Winnipeg church called
Skaptasson to be its minister. But new leaders were being
developed, for Rögnvaldur Pétursson of North Dakota and
Jóhann Solmundsson of Gimli enrolled at the Meadville
Theological School and Thorvaldur Thorvaldsson at Harvard.
R. Pétursson was to have a very great influence on the
movement.

In 1901 (June 16 and 17) The Unitarian Conference of
Icelandic Churches was organized in Gimli. Delegates came not
only from the congregations at Gimli and Winnipeg but from
many other places. Present also, from Chicago was the
Secretary of the Western Unitarian Conference, Dr. Franklin
C. Southworth. At the closing service Dr. Southworth
preached and christened several children, one of whom was
named in his honor — Benjamin Franklin Olson.

It is not my intent to relate the entire history of the liberal
religious movement among the Icelanders in Canada but will
only highlight some more interesting events and incidents from
this early period.

Women were delegates to the early annual conferences and
served on committees, but none seemed to have been an officer
or trustee. One of the most notable of these women was
Margaret J. Benedictsson, a suffragette as well as Unitarian,
who published her own periodical, **Freyja,** consisting in large
part of translated pieces by and about American sufragettes.

The conference assisted young men at Meadville, who in
addition to R. Pétursson and Solmundsson, were Guðmundur
Arnason (graduated in 1908 as a Cruft Fellow) and Albert
Edward Kristjánsson (1909 graduate).

Confirmation was an important rite in these churches for
young people fourteen and fifteen years of age. About 1915, the
Winnipeg Church's by-laws stated that "confirmation
automaticaly means membership or anyone can join at age 15,

but no one is eligible for office until age 18".

So here are my roots — a Prairie Unitarian. Life could be quite isolated on a Manitoba farm during the early part of this century and on through the depression. There was not much opportunity for travel. But the printed word opened up the wider world. My non-Unitarian grandfather was an avid reader, and a skeptic if not a free thinker. My other grandparents and my mother worked within the Unitarian context (both the church and the Ladies' Aid) to express their convictions. Ethics was at the heart of the beliefs in my home and was neither churchy nor dogmatic nor narrowly moralistic. But I now realize the important role of my prairie home environment, and not the least of this was the influence of the Icelandic Unitarian movement in Canada.

It also seems that the liberal religion of these pioneers was very much involved with the goals and dreams that they had for their beloved native Iceland. They wished for its independence and its prosperity. This is similar to the history of American Unitarianism and Universalism, which at its best has been in some sense an American "civil" or "national" religion, or as the late A. Powell Davies (a Britisher by birth) preferred to say, "American's Real Religion". So the Icelandic immigrants' religion and national goals were interrelated and indeed intertwined. The great Icelandic nationalist of the late 19th century, Matthías Jochumsson, was a liberal religionist and clergyman. It was he who on the occasion of the 100th anniversary of the settlement of Iceland, which was a time to express the spirit of independence from Danish colonialism, authored the national anthem. Obviously his somewhat conservative bishop had ambivalences toward him. He had spent time at Manchester College in England where he had hoped to study with Martineau, but he was ill. He considered William Ellery Channing one of the greatest minds of all times. The source for his strong conviction about an independent Iceland was the one and the same as those of his religious beliefs namely that the mind which was capable of rational thought as the source of truth must be free and unfettered. Jochumsson was for the country and for the countrymen abroad a national hero and for many he was a religious hero and inspiration as well. There is a parallel in Minnesota among the Norwegians where their greatest Unitarian leader Kristofer Janson was first known as a champion of the "landsmaal" or language of the common people and then secondly for his liberal religious views.

But this causes problems as far as the offspring and the grandchildren of the immigrants are concerned. My parents and my peers were Canadians first; our experience had all been Canadian, and we knew neither the mountains nor the salt water nor the midnight sun which are all parts of the national dream. But the older Icelandic Unitarians used their churches to preserve their vision of this heritage and language. The minutes of the Conference which was the core of the Western Canada Unitarian Conference were written in Icelandic until the very early 1950's. After a 20 year lapse it would appear to me, now an outsider, that the Icelandic consciousness has fared better than the Unitarian religious heritage in most cases; the exception I would note is the Unitarian Church of Arborg, the only surviving church. But I see some parallels for us, especially those who consider themselves sophisticated Americans. Our articulation of who we are is replete with references to the "founding fathers", and America's real religion, and abolition all American nationalistic themes. We project our national issues in our Unitarian-Universalism.

Having shared some rather specific personal reminiscences, allow me to make some generalizations. First, the prairies were alive politically and ideologically when I was a youth. Winnipeg was very much our center and was the hub of socialistic ideology. I remember the formal beginnings of the CCF party. J.S. Woodsworth and John Queen were heroes of mine because they cared for the plight of the common person with whom I identified. And this was the record of one of our Unitarian ministers about whom I heard a great deal from my grandmother, and who in fact served in the Manitoba legislature — Albert E. Kristjánsson. This populism and socialism and religion all came together for me when as an 18-year old youth I attended my first YPRU conference which featured Stephen H. Fritchman.

Secondly my ethnic background did cause an ambivalence. On the one hand it seemed that models to us were the Anglos (the English and Scottish of Manitoba),for everywhere they were in positions of power. On the other hand, I was truly interested in the Icelandic tradition, especially its poetry, its folk tales and sagas. I also was aware that my conversations with my maternal grandfather especially were far broader and deeper than any I could have with Anglo neighbors; in fact this was the case with most of the first generation neighbors. They were at home in discussions on Marx and socialism, and free thought as well as Christianity. And I have found the answer. In the libraries which I have inherited from my grandparents are a lot of periodicals from 1900 until 1940 published in Icelandic both in Iceland and Canada, and I have been amazed to find there articles on Freud, health foods, sufferage, etc. The big surprise when I was a college student was my grandfather asking me what I thought of Plato and engaging me in quite a conversation.

But alas, for most of my contemporaries who were also second and third generation Canadians, and raised in Unitarian homes, not only the ethnic emphasis of the churches was meaningless, but apparently also the other issues so alive for the immigrants. No connection was made with their lives and experiences which were far removed from the old country and the principles and philosophy of liberal religion as it applied to the immigrants. Most seem not to understand its essence and its evolutionary nature. Many times do I hear that the Lutheran churches today are now almost like the Unitarian church of their parents — but whether that is so or not, no one has chosen to ask about the changes in Unitarianism over the same period. The cop-out excuse so prevalent is that all the religions are at heart the same — they all try to do good; and of course in the past 25 years it has not been a particular asset in Canada to subscribe to an "American" religion.

The stage was undoubtedly set for a significant Unitarian movement among the Icelanders in Canada. At its heyday there were at least eight churches, five ministers and over 600 members. But it was more Icelandic perhaps than it was Unitarian. Perhaps the values, the outlook and the attitudes of the children and grandchildren and even great grandchildren of these pioneers have been influenced by this brand of Prairie Unitarianism. In my own current travels as an Interdistrict Representative I find in our churches and fellowships in

Regina, or Saskatoon, or Edmonton and even in the Twin Cities and Chicago and Long Island as well as in the Manitoba communities persons sharing this background, and many others who in conversation I find more than a nostalgia about their Unitarian background.

This is important to me. The little church at Lundar was sold in 1950's to the Canadian Legion for their clubrooms. They have outgrown it and moved, and today the building is a Goodwill store. Even the Ladies' Aid, the backbone, has gone out of existence. But there is still a Unitarian presence occasionally when a Unitarian minister officiates at the funeral service of one of the old stalwarts. And there are a few holdouts who have not been willing to join one of the churches of the area.

1. **Report of the Committee on Goals,** Boston: Unitarian Universalist Association, 1967, p. 40.

2. Albert R. & Emily M. Vail, **Heroic Lives in Universal Religion,** Boston: Beacon Press, 1917.

3. A personal letter to the author from the Rev. Albert E. Kristjansson, October 25, 1960.

4. Nina Draxten, **Kristofer Janson in America,** Northfield: Norwegian American Historical Association, 1976, p. 185.

5. P.M. Petursson, "The Unitarian Church of Winnipeg", a reprint from **The Icelandic Canadian,** Winnipeg: Spring, 1967.

6. A personal letter from Rev. Albert E. Kristjansson, February 6, 1961.

7. I heard this tale from the poet-farmer Guttormur J. Guttormsson at an Icelandic Festival ca. 1948.

8. Albert E. Kristjansson, February 6, 1961.

Appendix H

American Influences on The Beginnings of Unitarianism Among Icelanders in The United States and Canada*

A paper for presentation at
Collegium 1979
Craigville, Massachusetts
September 27, 1979
by V. Emil Gudmundson
UUA Interdistrict Representative

Unitarians and Universalists are often amazed to discover that there was at the turn of the century an active group of ethnic Unitarian churches in Canada and the United States which had their own conference, publications, church camp, hymnals and ministers and until about 1950 kept all their records in their native tongue. I refer of course to the Icelandic Unitarian churches, which were primarily in Manitoba. In the 1930's there were 8 congregations, a dozen "preaching stations" and 5 or 6 ministers.

Was this just an accident of history? True, the Unitarians had "missions" among the Norwegians, Finns and Swedes as well, but the most we have to show are a few isolated congregations without any embracing organization as among the Icelanders. I stated in 1975 that an "argument can be made that in no way could Unitarianism of the latter part of the 19th century help but become an influence among the Icelandic settlers in Canada and the U.S." [1] I am now even more convinced that this is the case.

A great many of the Icelandic settlers were ready heart and soul for the yeastiness of American thought in both religion

*Portions of this paper are paraphrased in Chapters 4 and 5, but it is included as an appendix to **The Icelandic Unitarian Connection** because it supplements the author's account of Björn Pétursson and Matthías Jochumsson.   GEB.

and politics which flourished in the latter half of the nineteeth century. There was as well a simultaneous ferment in literature and politics back in the old country which did affect religious thought. The writings of Channing and Martineau, for example, were known and respected.

The purpose of this paper is to explore a part of the influence on the Icelandic settlers which led to the formation of these Unitarian churches, and more specifically the American influence in the 1880's and 1890's. The emigration began in the early 1870's when settlers went to Ontario and Wisconsin. It became a large movement in 1875 when a colony or reserve was established on the western shores of Lake Winnipeg and called New Iceland. The same year a permanent settlement was established in Minnesota, and in 1878 settlers moved to northeastern North Dakota and elsewhere in Manitoba. All the while scores settled in Winnipeg, and it soon became the "headquarters" of Icelanders in the New World. Except for those in Winnipeg, the settlers engaged mainly in farming and some along Lake Winnipeg in fishing. It took a decade or so for men to enter the trades or business, and a little longer to enter professions, except for the clergy, who were very few in number. Most of the clergy were either educated in or "retooled" in Norwegian or German Lutheran seminaries in the U.S. and were much more orthodox and rigid in their beliefs than their old country counterparts.

It is against this background that one must understand the beginnings of liberal thought in religion among these settlers. There were no intellectuals in the academic sense leading them to radicalism and rationalism, but there were many self-educated and hightly intelligent people who soon reached out for new populist and radical ideas then present on the American scene.

One finds two American influences on these settlers, although they overlap, and are treated separately in this paper because a person is identified with each. First was the **Unitarian** influence through the person of Björn Pétursson, founder of the First Icelandic Unitarian Church of Winnipeg. Second was the influence of **Free Religion,** through the personage of Stephan G. Stephansson, who was to become a leading poet both in Canada and Iceland.

I. The Unitarian Influence — Björn Pétursson

In December 1886, the Rev. Grindall Reynolds, secretary of the American Unitarian Association in Boston, received a letter from Miss Jennie E. McCaine, a member of Unity Church in St. Paul and agent for the Post Office Mission for Minnesota, telling him about an Icelandic farmer in Pembina County in Dakota Territory who was interested in Unitarianism. 2 The man was Björn Pétursson, who became the founder of the Icelandic Church in Winnipeg in 1891, and in 1890 the husband of Miss McCaine. This appears to be the first contact between the A.U.A. and other American Unitarians with Icelanders in North Dakota and Manitoba, though this certainly was not the first contact Icelanders in their homeland had with Unitarianism. 3 Mr. Reynolds wasted little time in contacting the Rev. Kristofer Janson who was minister of a Norwegian Unitarian Church in Minneapolis and headed the A.U.A.'s Scandinavian mission in the Midwest. 4

Miss McCaine quotes quite extensively from a letter she had received from Pétursson. He wrote: "I am fully satisfied that I belong to your church, heart and soul... I recognize in the Unitarian movement the reformation I have long hoped for and expected and should be glad to get a chance to promote the same among my countrymen which on the whole are very intelligent people and not so priest-ridden and orthodox as their relatives the Norwegians." 5

This very first letter raises two questions which cannot be answered with any full documentation. One is, "How did Mr. Pétursson 6, a retired farmer, hear about the Post Office Mission and Unitarianism?" A second question is, "How did he gain command of the English language in correspondence?" For I am satisfied that the letters were written by him.

Mr. Pétursson was the son of a minister who served a parish in the sparsely populated area of east Iceland. He attended schools in the Reykjavík area for several years. He wrote Miss McCaine: "I was educated for the ministry in my own country Iceland but when I got through college I could not prevail on my conscience to preach dogmas I did not believe in myself so I gave it up." 7 His brother-in-law elaborates on this part of his life in his obituary. 8 According to Ólafsson, Pétursson had but one year left when the students rebelled against the rector, who was reinstated. Pétursson did not return, partly because he did not want to return to the same administration, but also "because his intent had been to prepare himself for the ministry, but at that time he had begun to question many of the church's teachings." 9 This would have been in 1846 when he was 20. The following year he married, and settled (down) to farming in east Iceland until 1870. During this period, to use his words, "in the old country (I) held offices of public trust, among them the membership of the legislature assembly for three successive terms (9 years)." 10 It could well be that his course of study included English in addition to Latin and Danish. It could also be that during his years of public service he was called upon to communicate in English. It is not necessarily surprising that he could read and speak English quite well, for this was commonplace among the early immigrants, but it was rarer that the immigrants mastered written English. Pétursson shows in his letters to Mr. Reynolds of the A.U.A. a good facility with the written language.

He may also have mastered it in the New World. He came to Canada in 1876 and "in three years I lost my whole property in the swamps of the Icelandic reserve on the west shore of Lake Winnipeg." 11 He moved his family to Pembina County, N.D. in 1879, took a year off to return to Iceland, and upon his return visited his son, Dr. Páll Björnsson, a physician in Houston, Minnesota prior to his death in 1881. His wife died in 1884, and he left the farm and divided his time with his childen who lived in Pembina County. He was then a man close to sixty, and one gets the impression, that except for his poverty, he would have been a gentleman farmer. He read voluminously, not only in his native tongue but in Norwegian, Danish and English. Somewhere he came across the Post Office Mission.

Petursson may have been an exception among his fellow Icelanders, but only in that he could apparently read and write English quite fluently. These settlers, however poor, and with backgrounds of meager formal education, nevertheless spent a lot of time reading and neighbors shared whatever books, periodicals and newspapers they received. Recycling reading matter was a fact of life.

After the initial contact with Miss McCaine, Pétursson wasted little time becoming a Unitarian missionary among the Icelanders. He had a lot of contact with Kristofer Janson, who also provided him with money from his "book fund" 12 to help translate and publish pamphlets. Janson had written three pamphlets in Norwegian for his own use 13 and sent copies to Pétursson. Mr. Pétursson's first letter to Mr. Reynolds of the A.U.A. gives a flavor of his enthusiasm and his work:

> Since March I have been engaged in your missionary work. According to an agreement with Rev. K. Janson, I have translated and caused to be printed some 3 of his many excellent pamphlets.. About 1500 of these I have already through the mail distributed to the various Icelandic settlements in Canada and in Minnesota. The remaining pamphlets I am just now busy in distributing in the wide Icelandic settlements in Pembina and Cavalier counties, D.T., my own locality, mostly walking from house to house, and lecturing where I can gather any number together. On the whole I have met with a better reception that I expected. Of course there are some orthodox fanatics who resist the new ideas with all their might... but they are pretty well matched with intelligent liberals, who already are, some half, some whole Unitarians, while the rest, the majority is indifferent, sunk in a dead or half-dead Christendom, if such a low religious state deserves so noble a name. 14

In the fall of 1887, Pétursson spent two months in Winnipeg, where the largest concentration of Icelanders was to be found. By then the community had a weekly newspaper, its own meeting place and many cultural groups as well as an Icelandic Lutheran congregation. He met with small groups of people in homes in various parts of the city, but the enthusiasm was apparently not overwhelming. He persisted. He lectured and discussed wherever he could get even a small audience and an example of this thought and themes is expressed in this report: The topics lectured on or discussed are following:

1 The theological doctrine of the Trinity, its origin, and lack of scriptural foundation.

2 What Christ did say about himself and the teaching of the apostles Paul and Peter concerning his personality.

3 Objections to the orthodox dogma of eternal punishment; Prayer having no effect on God, but benefiting and elevating oneself.

4 Othodoxy itself the principal cause of the growing unbelief, indifference and atheism among Christian peoples.

5 The noble aim of the liberal Christians, especially the Unitarians.

6 The trials and disasters afflicting humanity not directly by God as punishment but as a natural consequence of the human transgressions, ignorance and folly, according to divine law and order. 15

He repeated this method of "evangelizing" in his own Pembina County, and then the following spring in Lyon and Lincoln counties in Minnesota. Here is this older man going from home to home, and community to community preaching and promoting Unitarianism! He seemed to get more apathy than opposition. In a letter to Mr. Reynolds in 1888 he says the best news he has is organization of a "society, mostly of young men, for the purpose of investigating into religious matters and seeking general enlightenment and progress in all what constitutes a true manliness. This society, will, I am sure, be a great help to our cause in the future." 16

He was in Winnipeg again in the summer of 1888, and seemed to fare better in promoting "rational religion". He held his first two public lectures, the 1st on the question: "Is the Lutheran doctrine of justification by faith alone consistent with the teachings of Christ?" and the 2nd: "Is the doctrine of Trinity, the godhead of Jesu Christ and the Holy Ghost taught by Christ himself and his apostles?" 17 The weekly newspaper, **Lögberg**, reports that the attendance was rather small, but Pétursson was sufficiently encouraged by the response to make plans to move to Winnipeg and establish a Unitarian mission there.

It is not my purpose in this paper to detail Pétursson's missionary efforts and his organization of the Icelandic Unitarian Church; that is a separate story. But it is relevant to pursue further the influence of Unitarianism on Pétursson and to examine his own thoughts. There is but one sermon, extant, but he did write brief articles and numerous letters that give us some clues. He was a friend of Stephan G. Stephansson, whom we shall consider in Part II of this paper, and was thus conversant with the radical religious thought he represented. But he can perhaps best be classified as a rationalist who had an abiding interest in religion.

For some he was rather much of a radical. T.B. Forbush, then A.U.A. Western Superintendent writes of him:

> Peterson is a radical, almost, if not quite an ethical culturist...and he puts things in such ways that he is often called atheist, not only by the bigoted Lutherans but also by the more liberal.... P. is rough, untrained, extreme in some of his utterances, and under the influence of "Unity" and his wife is much more radical than the majority of his liberal countrymen. Thorsteinsson of Gimli, who heard him in April writes, "his sermon was more like to lead the people from the belief in any God at all, than leading them to Him." [18]

Later he says:

> He has no imagination, no religious sentiment, and he is aging very fast. He holds only one service on Sunday in the evening that is a dry argumentative discourse, fairly well written but poorly read. he uses no prayer except Lord's Prayer and benediction though he has hymns and Bible lessons. But the service is juiceless." [19]

It is interesting to note that Mr. Forbush refers to the "Unity" influence, which of course was a live controversy with him and the A.U.A. "Unity" referred to the Western Unitarian Conference office and its periodical, which was considered "ultra-radical". The A.U.A. and Mr. Forbush opened up a "competitive office" in Chicago. But the only related inference we have from Pétursson himself is a letter to Mr. Reynolds after attending the Annual Conference of the Minnesota Unitarian Conference in October 1888: "I was so favorably impressed with all what I saw and heard at St. Cloud that I desire to be formally accepted as a member of the (Western Conference) and admitted to the Unitarian ministry, if you consider me qualified to." [20]

But what about his own utterances? The one sermon extant is entitled **About the Divine Inspiration of the Bible,** [21] and is rather detailed in supporting the thesis that the Bible is a very human book. His conclusion is "that the prophecy of the Old Testament is not an iota more significant than prophecy of other cultures both early and recent."

In a letter to his friend Stephan G. Stephansson he rambles somewhat but opines:

> You say you are a Unitarian. I think that is a misunderstanding. What are you? Agnostic? Materialistic? Herbert and Huxley were really Unitarians, and even Ingersoll, though they call themselves Agnostics. They believe in the Oneness of the Universe; in some central, intelligent power i.e. the Unitarian God. They, because of some stubbornness, or arrogance, or eccentricity pretend not to know of this central power. But that is not true. They and we know almost as much about that as we do about many other things, e.g. life, mind, electricity, gravitation, magnetism, infinite time and space. The truth is, that no one knows all the truth about any of these things. ... **Unity** refers not only to the unity of God, but also to the unity of mankind in one faith, and one brotherhood. Unitarianism, modern Universalism and modern Judaism are in reality the same and must unite in time. [22]

In the foreward to a Janson pamphlet he translated he writes:

> Unitarians call themselves Christian believers in the Unity of God and they truly are. They believe in and pray to One God, the Creator and Almightly

Father. They believe in Christ, as the greatest of all
of God's sons and ambassadors among mankind.
They believe in the basic teachings of Christ: that
man is saved only by "doing the will of the Heavenly
Father" to love God and men as the great
commandment, and relevant both to this world and
the next. Unitarians would unite all Christians into
one society. They hope that this will be
accomplished when all the weeds are eradicated
which orthodoxy has sown in the Christian fields.
They have eternal faith in that truth which is in
Christianity. [23]

Pétursson seems to have believed in the institution of the
church to promote the truths of Christendom. He absorbed the
new thought shared by Stephansson, the radical thought of the
1880's but he never dismissed the concept of the church as the
vehicle for transmitting that thought. There may be some doubt
as there was among Forbush, Janson and even Stephansson
that he could ever build a church, but it was not because he did
not believe in the church. That is one reason that he translated
M.J. Savage's **Unitarian Catechism,** [24] and admonished people
to use it for teaching youth.

The Rev. Albert Kristjánsson, in reflecting upon Pétursson,
likened him to Channing for the Icelandic Unitarian
movement: "A rationalist he was, influenced by later thought
such as Ingersoll and Kristofer Janson. A pamphleteer he also
was. And in addition he was a missionary who never gave up
till he had breathed the last breath." [25]

II. The Free Thought Influence — Stephan G. Stephansson

The distinctive thought of late nineteenth century
America was humanistic in character…. The
humanistic outlook with emphasis on man as the
central and creative factor in the drama of life,
wedded to the sharpened sense of his place in
history, largely governed prevailing attitudes
toward the new historical sciences of geology and
evolutionary biology.

Stow Persons [26]

One would assume that this description of the American intellectual scene pertains to those in academic and scholarly pursuits whether in the academy, on the lecture circuit, among writers and publishers, or with some of the more progressive religious leaders. Persons is, in fact, referring to the intellectual climate in which the Free Religious Association developed which was organized in 1867 "to promote the interests of pure religion, to increase interest in the scientific study of theology and to increase fellowship in the spirit"... with the motto "Freedom and Fellowship in Religion." 27 The FRA flourished for most of the next two decades mainly in publishing and in the sponsorship of lectures.

Who would have thought that poor and struggling immigrant farmers in North Dakota would be reached by the ferment which the FRA represented? And these were immigrants for whom English was a new language. Björn Pétursson, who is the subject of the preceding section of this paper, was not alone in either the reading of English publications or in questioning the old tenets of Lutheranism, the religion of their homeland, Iceland. There were others who were just as interested and incisive, and one in particular became the "intellectual" leader of the Pembina County Icelanders, and later of all Icelanders in the U.S. and Canada, Stephan G. Stephansson.

Born in Iceland in 1853, of poor farm parents with keen intelligence, he was nevertheless destined to become recognized as one of Iceland's greatest poets. He had little opportunity for formal education, but in his own words he says: "Due to poverty of my parents the only books we had were the Bible and a few religious treatises, but I read everything I could lay my hands on, good or bad, depending largely upon the kindness of our neighbors. I became at the age of 15 a hired man to my uncle (and) it was my good fortune that he had a well-stocked library of which I took good advantage." 28 He reflected much later that in his youth he considered both the Bible and the Eddas divinely inspired.

At age 20 he set sail for the New World, arriving in Milwaukee, and spent the next year as a day laborer. With some money saved, he struck out with a bride to homestead in Shawano County, WI. Hardships continued, but he did not

relent in his reading. On his own he studied the English
language, and as a testament to this there is in his personal
library a well-worn copy of **The National Fourth Reader**
inscribed with his name and the date 7-4-74, below the name of
Rasmus B. Anderson, the great friend of Icelanders from whom
he apparently secured it. [29] Writing to a friend in 1890 he
opines, "One must read, otherwise we become nothing but belly
and mouth." [30]

In 1880 he moved to a new but larger Icelandic settlement in
North Dakota, Pembina County. Here he soon found old
friends, one of whom was a gifted and restless young Lutheran
minister, Páll Thorlaksson, who though a product of
Concordia Seminary in St. Louis and thus orthodox, was to
Stephansson a stimulating friend. Stephansson joined the
Lutheran church in his community when it was formed,
although he objected publicly to two Articles of the by-laws:
one regarding the Confessions, and the second to the exclusion
of women from the government of the church. Nevertheless he
served as Secretary, and in 1885 he was a delegate to the first
convention of the Icelandic Lutheran Synod. Here he fared no
better and subsequently withdrew his involvement in the
Lutheran church, to become one of its critics.

Apparently in 1885 he began to subscribe to **The Index**, the
weekly publication of the Free Religious Association, edited by
William J. Potter and B.F. Underwood. There is little use in
speculating how he made this contact. According to a writer of
the period, Thorstina Walters, many of these settlers knew
about and admired Robert G. Ingersoll for his address to the
Rupublican Convention in 1876 [31] but whether they knew his
free thought one can only guess. In any event, the Stephnsson
library, now housed in the Icelandic Collection at the
University of Manitoba, contains **The Index**, as well as several
other books indicating his obvious interest in radicalism and
free thought. [32]

Thus a rather poor immigrant farmer in North Dakota made
contact with the ferment of the new and radical intellectual
thought of America. In a letter to a friend in 1890 he lists nine
Free Thought pulications and evaluates them, and also adds
that he found good reading in the Popular Science and
Humboldt Library series. [33] And Stephansson found others in

the settlement who shared his views about traditional religion and its doctrines which discourage free inquiry. In the dead of winter in 1888 he and others gathered to organize the Icelandic Cultural Society, but let his own account which he wrote for the weekly in Winnipeg, **Lögberg**, relate this story:

Humanity, Research, Freedom. The objectives of this organization are to support and promote culture and ethics, that ethics and that faith which is based upon experience, knowledge and science. In place of ecclesiastical sectarianism it seeks humanitarianism and fellowship; in place of unexamined confessions of faith, sensible and unfettered research; in place of blind faith, independent convictions; and in place of ignorance and superstition, spiritual feedom and progress on which no fetters are placed. 34

He then continued with this commentary:

This society was organized last February 4, by 7 men... It was the opinion of the charter members that most organizations which either enslave men to ancient ideas, or attempt to erect narrow bounds for study and thinking, were not capable of meeting today's greatest need: free inquiry and self education. The ideas and opinions of those who join the society are never dictated by the members, however few may belong, for the society's objective is to give mutual support and encouragement for each member to become better informed and morally stronger without any restrictions as to what one may accept or reject. It is expected that the membership will divide into groups which shall each take different and specific areas of inquiry, and especially those which concern the common weal. These types of societies have been established in several places in this country, and have prospered though they are relatively new and small numerically. Prof. F. Adler of New York is the founder. 35

It would seem that Stephanson has a very general interpretation of the Ethical Culture Societies for they were hightly structured, much more than the Icelandic Cultural Society could hope to be. Article III of the Certificate of Inauguration of the New York Society, February 21, 1877 reads:

> The object of said society will be the mutual improvement in religious knowledge and the furtherance of religious opinion, which shall be in part accomplished by a system of weekly lectures, in which the principles of ethics shall be developed, propagated, and advanced among adults, and in part by the establishment of a school or schools wherein a course of moral instruction shall be supplied for the young. 36

Since Stephansson was reading **The Index,** the model for the Icelandic Cultural Society could have as well been the Liberal or Free Religious Clubs that were to be found throughout cities in the Northeast and Middle West at that time. And it is worthy of note that the Statement of Objectives of the Icelandic Cultural Society resembles that of the FRA which appeared in every issue of **The Index:** "The objects of this Association are to encourage the scientific study of religion and ethics, to advocate freedom in religion, to increase fellowship in the spirit, and to emphasize the supremacy of practical morality in all the relations of life." 37

The society prospered for the next 2-3 years. Stephansson was the secretary and kept detailed records. The By-laws are relatively simple. 34 names are listed on the membership roll among them two men who were to touch the Unitarian story quite closely: Björn Pétursson, missionary and founder of the Icelandic Unitarian Church of Winnipeg; and Skapti Brynjólfsson, a N.D. State Senator from 1891 to 1893 and the third president of the Winnipeg church. Members took turns in the preparation of papers on such topics as Natural History, Comparative Religion and Mythology, and History of Religions. Guest speakers were occasionally featured. Pétursson spoke on Unitarianism. Stephansson gave a public lecture on the thought of Robert G. Ingersoll. The Society also established a modest library and some recorded titles were: **Bible Myths; Kingdoms of Nature; Childhood of Man; Childhood Religions; The North American Review.** 38 The Society was attacked in the pages of the Lutheran monthly, **Sameining** 39 as infidel and unchristian, and Stephanson became engaged in lengthy debates with the editor, the Rev. Jón Bjarnason, who even asserted that one of the major problems in America was the support and encouragement of unrestricted religious liberty. Very few Icelanders in the New World could miss this dialogue for it took place in the pages of the weekly newspapers, **Lögberg** and **Heimskringla**, and it made the ground more fertile for the development of an Icelandic Unitarian movement.

The efforts of the Icelandic Cultural Society were short-lived, for it disbanded in 1893 without any groups being formed in other settlements. One major reason was that several of the leading members moved away, among them Stephansson who resettled in the foothills of the Canadian Rockies, some 80 miles north of Calgary. Others went to Winnipeg and Seattle and Alberta. But a tremendous impact had been made on the Icelanders. It was for Pétursson and others to try to organize missions for the Unitarians in North Dakota and Winnipeg, with success coming with the establishment of the Icelandic Unitarian Church of Winnipeg in 1891.

Stephansson, the Poet

Stephansson's contribution to liberal religious thought among the Icelanders would have been great even had it been restricted to the Icelandic Cultural Society. Always the individualist, he never joined a Unitarian church, but his ideas and his outlook on life as well as his concern for the commonweal were to find expression in poetry which he wrote primarily from his Alberta farm home at night after work on the fields and the stables had been completed.

It is difficult to speak of the poetry of Stephan G. Stephansson without using superlatives. Professor Watson Kirkconnel of the University of Toronto has called him Canada's leading poet; Professor Frank S. Cawley of Harvard University considered him "the greatest poet of the western world." .... There can be no doubt that Stephan G. Stephansson has enriched Icelandic literature immeasurably and deserves therefore to be ranked with the greatest poets (Iceland) has produced. When one considers that Stephansson had practically no formal schooling, was a farmer all his life, was a pioneer three times, raised a large family, and was able to study and compose only after wresting a living as a day laborer or farmer at the expense of sleepless nights, his energy and genius are the more surprising. .... The creative urge was so strong within him that fatigue and occasionally even gaunt hunger were forgotten as he sat alone reading, thinking and composing. When he finally collected his poems, he published them under the title **Andvokur,** meaning "sleepless or restless nights." [40]

Much has been made of the strong influence that his native Iceland had on him for his poetry is filled with allusions to the sagas of old, to the traditions of the country and to the scenery and landscape. He also wrote in the Icelandic poetic tradition with richness of diction and alliteration and in a style which was very Icelandic, although he was also in some ways very original. but the matter of content and ideas can better be understood if one is informed by knowledge of the radical thinking in religious and political circles in the United States during the latter part of the 19th century, and especially an acquaintanceship with the Free Religious movement. An individualist, he never rejoined any church, but had an affinity to Unitarianism, and in fact willed that a Unitarian service be used for his funeral. [41]

This aspect of the influence upon Stephansson and his writings has yet to be studied thoroughly, but a good start has been made by a scholar at the University of Iceland, Oskar O. Halldorsson. [42] In a dissertation on one of Stephansson's early collection of poems, he explores the apparent affinity he had for the ideas of Felix Adler, and draws some parallels, using quotations from Adler's **Creed and Deed.** It is worth noting some of the examples used. The translations used of Stephansson's poems are quite accurate but their original vigor is somewhat lost.

ADLER

Attitude Towards Life:
The dead are not dead, if we have loved them truly. In our own lives we give them immortality. .... All the good that was in them lives in you, the germ and the nucleus of the better that shall be.
— **Creed and Deed,** page 35, 1894 ed.

Heaven is on this Earth
And now the new Ideal differs from Christianity in this, that it seeks to approach the goal of a Kingdom of Heaven upon earth, not by the miraculous interference of the Deity, but by the laborious exertion of men, and the slow but certain progress of certain generations.
— **Creed and Deed,** page 96

Attitude Toward Christ
It was the humanity, not the dogma of Jesus, by which Christianity triumphed.
— **Creed and Deed,** page 163

Progress:
Far from being exemplary, the ideas of right and wrong entertained by our earliest progenitors were infinitely below our own ... Each age added its own to the stock of virtue, each contributed its share to swell the treasure of mankind.
— **Creed and Deed,** page 73 - 74

STEPHANSSON

The kindness never will be spoiled or spent;
The spool of time will keep the thread intact.
Though visions for thy glory with thee went,
The ones you gave inspired so much I lacked.
— **Gestur** the poet's son killed by lightning 43

We see in each fact, not the fable
As feebly we search and appraise,
That law, if illucid, is stable
And leaves but one prospect to face;
To think not in hours, but in ages,
At eve not to claim all our wages
Will bring out the best in the race.
— **Brothers' Destiny** 44

No horns were blown nor havoc made
When He was in the Manger laid.
No diary the date has shown; His
His date of birth is still unknown.
His catechism was common toil,
His copy-book the living soil.
Where nature, old, yet all abloom,
In every knoll concealed a tomb.
— Eloi Lamma Sabahkthani 45

Wisdom, goodwill, goodness, perfection
are in no way innate to humanity from
creation; they only come from the heavy, lashing experiences of succeeding generations.
— Letters and Essays 46

The conclusion is fairly obvious and can be stated simply. The early Icelandic settlers were emigrating from a land beset by concerns about its future, not only because of the hardships inflicted by nature, but also because of the yoke of Danish rule which inhibited their natural tendency to freedom and individualism. A few like Stephan G. Stephansson found their way to literature in the new World that represented their values and spoke to their experiences. The match of Stephansson with the Free Religious Association was a good one. He, like many in the FRA, was suspicious of organizations for he was first and foremost an individualist; this is a characteristic which Persons believes helped to lead to the demise of the FRA as a thriving organization. However, because of his writings, whether poetry, essays or letters, he had a great influence on many of his fellow Icelandic settlers. He was also a friend of Unitarianism, and significantly his influence was perhaps the greatest during the first decade or so of the Icelandic Unitarian movement (1887-1900). Then the leaders, at least, spoke without hesitation about the Unitarian ideology or faith first, and its Icelandic component second which was to preserve the heritage. Stephansson's influence played no little part in this.

And the Unitarian missionary, Björn Pétursson was his neighbor and close friend, engaging in some very candid correspondence in which he states that he considers Stephansson an almost atheist, while he himself prefers to be a liberal Christian. But these two men were on the scene at the right time.

From Oskar O. Halldorsson, **Á Ferð og Flugi eftir Stephan G. Stephansson;**

Summary

Stephan G. Stephansson, the poet, was born at Kirkjuholl, Skagafjord, in the North of Iceland in 1853. At the age of twenty he emigrated together with his parents and some other relatives to America where he settled as a farmer in the State of Wisconsin. He lived there until 1880, when he moved to Pembina County, North-Dakota, where

he became a settler for the second time. He lived
there until 1889, when he moved again, this time to
Canada. He became a settler for the third time,
building his farm near the foot of the Rocky
Mountains in the Province of Alberta. There he
found peace of mind until he died in 1927.

Stephansson did not receive any schooling, but of
his own accord he acquired such knowlege and
maturity that he must be ranked among highly
educated people. He was only young when he
started writing poetry, but he did not write much
until his late thirties. At that time, however, his
poems began to appear in Icelandic publications in
America, establishing Stephansson firmly as a great
poet for the rest of his life. To his posterity he left a
large collection of poems, in addition to a number
of letters, essays, and newspaper articles.

Stephan G. Stephansson wrote only in Icelandic,
and is considered one of the greatest poets in the
history of Icelandic literature. His collections of
poems he called **Andvökur** ("Hours of
Sleeplessness"). The name suggests that this great,
but poor, settler-farmer had seldom any other time
than the night at the close of a hard day's work in
which he could devote himself to his literary
pursuits.

A Ferð og Flugi (On the Move) is narrative
poetry, based on the poet's recollections of his
travels through the early settlements of Canada
during the last two or three decades of the 19th
century. The travel episodes are not inter-
dependent, but all the same they serve as a
framework for the essence of the whole: the life and
destiny of Ragnheiður, the daughter of Icelandic
immigrants. In her youth she works to support her
father and younger brothers, as her father cannot
find work in the city. Her loyalty and filial respect is
vividly depicted. Later on, when her parents do not
need her help any more, the ties between her and her
family break and she passes away from her fellow-

countryfolk to the gay life of the city. Many years elapse. The poet finds out on one of his journeys that Ragnheiður has gone astray and has been excluded from the company of people who make pretensions to respectability. A striking event reveals, however, that she is still the same at heart. She dies as a heroine after having risked her life in an attempt to save a child from death.

"I was trying to depict the modern counterpart of the girl to whom Jesus is supposed to have said:"Woman, I won't condemn you either". These were the poet's own words in a letter he wrote. The purpose of the poem is to show that Ragnheiður was not in full command of her destiny. There was a variety of forces at work here. It was not enough, therefore, to describe Ragnheiður the individual. A clear picture of the environment which had formed her character and determined her destiny had to be drawn. Consequently, the poem as a whole is above all a description of local conditions at a particular time. But the poet does not only show us the frontier settlements and acquaint us with the struggle and the humble conditions of the settlers, but delves below surfaces to explore the currents which stir the ordinary patterns of human life and characterise the spirit of the age. Here the poet finds an occasion for satire, attacking with equal force social trends and the church which had undertaken the spiritual guidance of the people. At the same time, we can trace his steadfast belief in the inherent goodness of man together with optimistic hope of a better and richer life, when everyone will reach some degree of spiritual maturity.

In form **On the Move** is reminiscent of the ancient epics. The same metre is employed from beginning to end, and the progress of the narrative is fairly even and rather slow. The story, however, is rather disjointed in places because of the varied description which the poet gives of what passes before the traveller's eyes and his expression of views and emotions. A large part of the poem is therefore lyrical by nature. The poet has also mastered the method of dramatizing the style by putting words in the mouths of his characters. But whatever method he uses, the narrative always assumes a great sense of reality. There are few flashes of gaiety or humour, but various digressions and references to contemporary society reveal sarcasm. According to Stephansson himself, he deliberately chose the loose form of the travel narrative where all digressions were permissible.

The artistic quality of the poem is possibly at its best in descriptive passages on nature and human character. The configuration of the countryside looms in the background of every event. One can even hear the sounds of the weather. To the poet, such descriptive passages are an end in themselves. The same can be said of his analyses of character, which show how successfully he has managed to reveal human traits engendered by past experience.

On the Move was first published in Reykjavik in 1900. The poem attracted great attention in Iceland, where its author was little known at the time. It was reviewed with mixed feelings at first, but its popularity has been increasing in recent years, fulfilling the poet's hope:

"The truth one intended to tell will emerge of its own accord some time."

NOTES

1. "I Was Born A Prairie Unitarian", a paper delivered at the Annual Meeting of the Western District of the Canadian Unitarian Council, 1975

2. This letter is in the A.U.A. Secretary's book, now located in the Archives o the Andover Harvard Library. Most of the letters and repots referred to in this paper are from this collection.

3. The great Icelandic nationalist, poet, and clergyman, Matthias Jochumsson, relates in his autobiography, **Sogukaflar Af Sjalfum Mer,** that prior to 1871 he had been loaned the **Works of W.E. Channing** and had read them thoroughly. In 1873 he had made plans to visit at length with the Rev. James Martineau, but because of Martineau's illness he changed his plans and instead spent several weeks with another Unitarian minister, the Rev. Robert Spears, 73 Angell St. Brixton.

4. See Nina Draxten: **Kristofer Janson in America** Twayne Publishers 1976

5. Letter of Petursson to McCaine, A.U.A. Secretary's book, Dec. 2, 1886

6. The Icelandic spelling is "Pétursson", but whenever he corresponded with non-Icelanders he used Peterson.

7. Letter in 5 above.

8. **Heimskringla,** a weekly newspaper in Winnipeg, Sept. 30, 1893, page 1 an obituary written by Jón Ólafsson, Mr. Pétursson's brother-in-law and first president of the Icelandic Unitarian Church of Winnipeg.

9. McCaine to Reynolds Dec. 2, 1886

10. **Ibid**

11. **Ibid**

12. Report from Kistrofer Janson to Reynolds, Feb. 24, 1887.

13. The Icelandic titles are: **Guð Gyðinga og Guð Kristinna Manna** (The Jewish God and the Christian God); **Fagnaðar Boðskapur Hinna Othodoxu og Hinna Liberölu** (The Glad Tidings of the Orthodox and the Liberals); **Um Þrenningarlærdóminn og Guðdóm Krists** (The Trinity and the Deity of Christ). All were published in Winnipeg in 1887.

14. Pétursson to Reynolds, Dec. 31, 1887.

15 Peterson to Reynolds, Dec. 31, 1887. A.U.A. Letterbooks.

16. Pétursson to Reynolds, March 31, 1888. Here has reference to the Icelandic Cultural Society, treated in Part II of this paper.

17. Pétursson to Reynolds.

18. Forbush to Reynolds, May 26, 1892

19. Forbush to Reynolds, June 25, 1892.

20. Pétursson to Reynolds, Oct. 11, 1888.

21. **Dagsbrun,** a periodical March 1893.

22. Letter to Stephan Stephansson, March 19, 1892. In Bréf til Stephans G. Stephansson ed. by Finnbogi Gudmundsson, Reykjavik 1971. vol. 2.

23. **Un Þrenningarlærdóminn** pp 1-2 (Regarding Trinitarianism)

24. **Unitar Katkismus,** pamphlet 1891

25. Personal letter to the author dated Oct. 25, 1960.

26. **Stow Persons, Free Religion, An American Faith** New Haven Yale University Press. pp. 130-131

27. Charles Lyttle, **Freedom Moves West** Boston Beacon Press 1952 p. 123

28. **Icelandic Canadian Magazine,** Summer 1973 pp. 15-17

29. **Icelandic Canadian Magazine,** Spring 1974 pp. 17-21

30. Stephan G. Stephansson, **Bref og Rit,** vol. I, Reykjavik, 1939 p 11

31. Thorstina Waltes, **Modern Sagas,** N: D: Institute for Regional Studies p 120

32. Stephan G: Stephansson, **Bref og Rit,** vol I p. 10

The following names of periodicals and books indicate some of the reading done by Stephansson: **The New Ideal** (Boston); **Boston Investigator; Iron Clad Age** (Indianapolis); **Truth Seeker** (New York); **Free Thought** (San Fransisco); **Secular Thought** (Toronto); **The Twentieth Century** (New York); **The Individualist** (Denver); **Freethinker's Magazine** (Buffalo). He also recommends B.F. Underwood's **Debates and Essays** a well read copy is in his personal library.

33. **Ibid** vol. I p. 10

34. **Ibid** vol. IV p. 153

35. **Ibid**

36. Letter from Khoren Arisian, Leader of the New York Society for Ethical Culture, Nov. 1977.

37. Stow Persons, **Free Religion,** cited above. page 54.

A further parallel can be found in the following **Index** statement

THE INDEX

Boston, May 14, 1885

The ojects of THE INDEX may be defined by the objects of the Free Religious Association; namely, "To promote the practical interests of pure religion, to increase fellowship in the spirit, and to encourage the scientific study of man's religious nature and history"; in other words Righteousness, Brotherhood, and Truth. And it seeks these ends by the method of perfect Liberty of Thought. It would subject the traditional authority of all special religions and alleged revelations-the Christian no less than others-to the judgment of scientific criticism and impartial reason. It would thus seek to emancipate Religion from bondage to ecclesiastical dogmatism and sectarianism, in order that the practical power of religion may be put more effectually to the service of a higher Morality and an improved Social Welfare.

38. This information comes from the official Secretary's records of Íslenzka Menningarfelag now in the Icelandic Collection at the Dafoe Library, University of Manitoba.

39. **Sameining** monthly publication of the Icelandic Lutheran Synod from 1886 on.

40. Loftur Bjarnason, **Anthology of Modern Icelandic Literature** Beverly, California, University Extension Service, University of California, Vol. II 1961 pp. 215-216.

41. **Lögberg,** Feb. 1927.

42. Oskar O. Halldorsson, **Á Ferð og Flugi eftir Stephan G. Stephansson** Reykjavik, 1961, pp. 71-73. Also see Appendix I.

43. Translated by Paul Bjarnason, **More Echoes,** p. 15

44. Translated by Paul Bjarnason, **Odes and Echoes,** p. 118

45. Translated by Paul Bjarnason, **Odes and Echoes,** p. 109

46. **Bref og Rit** cited in 30 above.

Appendix I

Icelandic Unitarian Churches in North America

Stefan M. Jonasson
408 Amherst Street
Winnipeg, Manitoba
Canada, R3J 1Y9
10 March 1984

Barbara Gudmundson
5505 28 Avenue South
Minneapolis, Minnesota
USA, 55415

Dear Barbara,

John Gilbert* has asked me to forward you a list of historic Icelandic Unitarian congregations in North America. The following list includes all of the localities of which I am aware, though I am not altogether certain that the listing is complete. I have tried to provide a few background notes on each congregation.

WINNIPEG: The first Unitarian congregation among the Icelanders in North America was organized in Winnipeg in February, 1891 as the First Icelandic Unitarian Church of Winnipeg. In 1920, the First Icelandic Unitarian Church merged with the Winnipeg Tabernacle (Tjaldbudin), and Icelandic New Theology congregation, to form the First Federated Church of Unitarians and Other Liberal Christians. In 1945, the First Federated Church merged with the All Souls Church, and English speaking Unitarian congregation which did in fact have a significant anglophone Icelandic membership. The legal name of the Winnipeg church is still the First Federated Church, etc., though it came to be known as

*Rev. John Gilbert, minister, U.U. church of Winnipeg, Manitoba.

the First Unitarian Church and eventually the Unitarian Church of Winnipeg. There is still a significant Icelandic element in the church.

GIMLI: The Lutheran congregation at Gimli withdrew from the Icelandic Lutheran Synod of America in 1891 following Rev. Magnus Skaptason's "Easter Sermon". The Gimli congregation joined in the creation of the Icelandic Free Church Association in America, which applied for affiliation with the American Unitarian Association. After Skaptason was called to the Winnipeg church in 1894, the congregation fell into disarray while the Lutherans regrouped. In 1904, the Gimli Unitarian Church was organized. Following the merger in Winnipeg of First Icelandic Unitarian and the Tabernacle, the Gimli Unitarians adopted the 'Federated' name and became the First Federated Church of Gimli. In the 1950's, the church came to be popularly called Gimli Unitarian Church. The last reference to the Gimli Church in the UUA **Directory** was in 1975, when 23 members were reported. The church was, in fact, already inactive by the early 1970's. A legal organization still exists to administer the church property which consists of a spired church building on a double lot near the harbour area.

ARNES: As in Gimli, the Arnes congregation withdrew from the Lutheran Synod at the time of the "Easter Sermon" after which it fell into disarray. Arnes Unitarian Church was organized in 1909, becoming Arnes Federated Church in the 1920's. In 1954, the church reported 21 members and appears to have become dormant about this time. In 1968, the Arnes church building was moved to the Hnausa Unitarian Camp. The original organ from the Arnes church is on display at the Gimli Museum.

HNAUSA: The Breiduvik Congregation at Hnausa withdrew from the Lutheran Synod in 1891 only to meet the same fate as Gimli and Arnes. Hnausa Unitarian Church was organized in 1909 and was served by Rev. Rognvaldur Petursson until 1922. Nothing is known about the congregation beyond this point. Hnausa is also the site of Hnausa Unitarian Camp, a fresh air camp organized by the Western Canada Alliance of Unitarian Women in 1938.

RIVERTON: The First Federated Church of Riverton was organized in 1925. The last report to the denomination in 1955 indicated a membership of 38. Since that time, the membership has been absorbed by the Arborg Unitarian Church. A legal organization still exists to administer the small church building and property, and the UUA **Directory** continues to list Riverton (erroneously named 'Roberton') as an inactive society.

HECLA: Hecla was the site of Skaptason's "Easter Sermon". The Mikleyjar (Big Island) Congregation withdrew from the Lutheran Synod in 1891 and appears to have dissolved within a very short time. A Unitarian preaching station was maintained over the years, as was a Unitarian Ladies Aid group. The Hecla preaching station was served by Rev. Rognvaldur Petursson from 1917 to 1922, and again from 1937 to 1939. The Hecla Church, formerly owned by the Lutheran Church and currently owned by the Manitoba government, was built with the assistance of Unitarian contributions. Accordingly, a joint use agreement was made between Hecla Lutherans and Unitarians.

ARBORG: The Arborg Federated Church was organized in 1923. As with the other churches, the Arborg congregation has come to be known popularly as the Arborg Unitarian Church. An active congregation still exists at Arborg, as does a Ladies Aid group. The Arborg Unitarians have been active in the administration of the Hnausa Unitarian Camp.

LUNDAR: A church was established here in 1931. The Unitarian Church building from Mary Hill was moved to Lundar at a later date. The last known denominational contact with Lundar was in 1952, when 48 members were reported. A number of individual Unitarians still reside in the district.

OAK POINT: There are conflicting stories concerning the organization at Oak Point. Some suggest that the congregation was organized circa 1920. Philip Petursson maintains that 1930 is closer to the mark. We do know that Rev. Gudmundur Arnason served this church from 1929 to 1943. The church building was originally used at Otto (Shoal Lake). 2 The church appears to have lingered on until about 1950. Nothing is known beyond this point other than the fact that there are still a few Unitarians in the area.

OTTO (SHOAL LAKE): This congregation was established in 1909, and at one time had over 60 members. Otto, also known as Ljosvaka, maintained a church building for many years. Rev. Gudmundur Arnason served this congregation until 1943. The Otto Church is sometimes referred to as the Shoal Lake congregation. Rev. Halldor Johnson served Shoal Lake, Lundar and Oak Point until his death in 1950. Since that time, many people have moved out of the area which is quite desolate and sparsely populated. It is thought that the Otto congregation dissolved in the 1940's.

MARY HILL: The Mary Hill congregation was organized in 1908 and at one time had about 40 members. Rev. Gudmundur Arnason served the church from 1929 to 1943, during which time the building was moved to Lundar along with the congregation. It is, in fact, difficult to sort out many of the Unitarian congregations in the Western Interlake area since there was a great deal of overlap between them. Mary Hill and Lundar, in particular, often appear nearly indistinguishable. This is no doubt complicated by their having been served by the same minister in a circuit. The records for Mary Hill appear to have been lost, but it is thought that the congregation was absorbed by Lundar in the 1930's or 1940's.

HOVE: Hove is very near Otto. A preaching station was established here, served by Rev. Albert E. Kristjansson from 1917 to 1926. Nothing is known beyond this.

PINEY (PINE VALLEY): A preaching station was established here circa 1899 by Rev. Magnus Skaptason when he moved to Roseau, Minnesota. Rev. Rognvaldur Petursson made frequent visits here from 1921 to 1940, and Unitarianism appears quite strong in the area despite its isolation. It is known that Unitarian contributions were used to build a community church which was open to Unitarian use.

VOGAR (HAYLAND): A preaching station was established here, served by Arnason from 1935 to 1943. Little is known other than this except that Unitarian funds were again used to erect a community church which was used by local Unitarians.

REYKJAVIK: A small preaching station which appears to have been tied in with the Vogar station.

STEEP ROCK: Another small preaching station also served by Arnason from 1935 to 1943.

LANGRUTH: A preaching station on the west side of Lake Manitoba. Little is known about this station beyond their participation at the 1923 Icelandic Conference meeting.

SELKIRK: The Selkirk Lutheran congregation was divided following Skaptason's "Easter Sermon". The congregation did withdraw from the Lutheran Synod in 1892. There was a floundering group there for two or three years, but the Unitarians were never able to establish a permanent presence.

VIDINES (HUSAVIK): The Vidines Congregation withdrew from the Lutheran Synod in 1891. The congregation eventually returned to the Lutherans, but a number of individual residents in the Husavik district maintained an affiliation with the Unitarians and were often represented at Iclandic Conference meetings. Many Husavik Unitarians became members of the Gimli Unitarian Church. (John Gilbert is dedicating two babies at Husavik this very weekend!)

ICELANDIC UNITARIAN CONGREGATIONS IN SASKATCHEWAN:

WYNYARD: Wynyard was organized as the Quill Lake Church in 1906. An Icelandic New Theology congregation closely tied to the Winnipeg Tabernacle, the Quill Lake Church withdrew from the Lutheran Synod in 1910. The congregation was reorganized as the Wynyard Federated Church in 1921. The Wynyard Church was numerically the most important Icelandic Unitarian church behind the First Federated Church in Winnipeg. Wynyard Federated Church last appears in the UUA **Directory** in 1975 when in excess of 50 members were reported. Though now inactive, a few services have been held in Wynyard over the past few years. The church building was recently declared to be a 'Heritage Site'by provincial authorities, and the UUA has contacted local Unitarians concerning possible re-affiliation. The other Saskatchewan Icelandic Unitarian churches/preaching stations historically looked to Wynyard for leadership.

KANDAHAR: Established in the early 1920's, this church was served by Kristjansson from 1927 to 1928 and by Rev. Rognvaldur Petursson from 1929 to 1936.

KRISTNES (FOAM LAKE): The Kristnes story parallels Kandahar.

GRANDY, DAFOE and LESLIE: All three settlements maintained preaching stations which were serviced from Wynyard. The exact dates of existence are unknown, though these stations were active throughout the 1920's.

ICELANDIC UNITARIAN CONGREGATIONS IN THE UNITED STATES:

BLAINE, WASHINGTON: The Icelandic Free Church in Blaine was organized by Rev. Albert E. Kristjansson in 1928. Kristjansson served the church as minister from 1933 to 1943 and from 1946 to 1949. Now called the Free Church Unitarian, the Blaine congregation has been able to maintain ministerial services of one form or another up to the present day. With 30 members at present, the Blaine congregation has diversified its membership, expanding beyond its Icelandic base to include members from Blaine's larger community and White Rock, British Columbia.

SEATTLE: The Icelandic Liberal Church, also known as the Icelandic Liberal Unitarian Society, was organized by Kristjansson in 1928. Kristjansson served the congregation from 1928 to 1941 (as well as the First Church in Seattle from 1931 to 1932). Ties with the First Unitarian Church were always close, and it is my understanding that the Icelandic Liberal Church was absorbed by the First Church in the 1940's.

ROSEAU, MINNESOTA: An Icelandic Unitarian congregation was organized by Rev. Magnus Skaptason at Roseau circa 1899. The Roseau congregation had delegates at the 1903 Icelandic Unitarian Conference. However, by the 1923 conference, the congregation seems to have dissolved, though the nearby Piney congregation was represented then.

OTHER AREAS OF ACTIVITY: Before the turn of the century, especially in the early 1890's, it is known that there was Unitarian missionary activity among the Icelanders at Minneota, Minnesota and the surrounding area in Lincoln and Lyon counties. There is also reference to "North Dakota" delegates at the early Icelandic Conference meetings. These delegates were from the Hallson and Mountain areas in Pembina County. While there does not appear to have been any congregations per se in these areas, there was a Unitarian presence, much like Vidines (Husavik) and Selkirk in Manitoba. It is known, as well, that Rev. Rognvaldur Petursson spoke frequently at the Alberta Church in Markerville, and Icelandic Lutheran congregation which was in sympathy with the New Theology movement. It also seems likely that there were more preaching stations in Saskatchewan than have been noted, though I am not certain. Churchbridge (Thingvalla) and Tantallon (Holar and Vallarbygd) would be possible locations if such were the case.

There were, over the course of the years, also a number of conference meetings, four being especially significant. These conference meetings are noted below.

1891: A meeting was convened by Rev. Magnus Skaptason to found 'The Icelandic Free Church Association in America'.

Congregations represented at the initial meeting were Gimli, Vidines (Husavik), Arnes, Breiduvik (Hnausa) and Mikleyjar (Hecla). Selkirk joined the association the next year. The association, formed after the division created by Skaptason's "Easter Sermon", applied for affiliation with the American Unitarian Association in 1892, though the group was frankly more universalist than unitarian in its theology. It is interesting to note that only two of the New Iceland Lutheran congregations did not withdraw from the Lutheran Synod at this time, namely the Fraternal (Braedra) Congregation at Riverton and the Fljotshlidar Congregation at Geysir.

1901: A meeting was convened by Rev. Magnus Skaptason in June to found 'The Western Icelandic Unitarian Free Church Association'. The meeting, held at Gimli, had delegates present from Winnipeg, Roseau, Lundar, Gimli, Arnes, Hnausa, Hecla and North Dakota (Hallson and Mountain).

1903: A follow-up to the 1901 meeting was held in Winnipeg from July 30 to August 2. The name of the association was changed to 'The Western Icelandic Unitarian Church Association'. Delegates were present from all of the locations represented at the 1901 meeting along with delegates representing Husavik, Piney and Shoal Lake.

1923: Following the merger of the First Icelandic Unitarian Church of Winnipeg and the Winnipeg Tabernacle, a meeting was convened to organize an association of Unitarian and New Theology congregations. After an exploratory meeting at Wynyard in 1921, a conference was convened in Winnipeg in June of 1923 to form 'The United Conference of Icelandic Churches'. Delegates were present representing Winnipeg, Gimli, Arnes, Otto, Arborg, Quill Lake (Wynyard) as well as a number of delegates at large. Thirteen congregations formed the initial membership namely Winnipeg, Arborg, Hnausa, Arnes, Gimli, one unknown New Iceland congregation (Hecla or Riverton?), Mary Hill, Otto, Piney, Langruth, Wynyard, Kandahar and Kristnes.

I hope that the above summary is what you are looking for. I have enclosed two maps to indicated the relative location of congregations in Manitoba, Saskatchewan and Minnesota. The Icelandic Unitarian influence was, of course, not limited to these 'Icelandic' congregations. Their influence has been felt by all of the congregations in Western Canada District, as well as a number of congregations in Minnesota (Minneapolis-St. Paul and Duluth in particular) and the Victoria-Vancouver-Seattle triangle on the Pacific Coast. If I can be of further assistance to you, please do not hesitate to contact me.

Sincerely,
Stefan M. Jonasson3

1. "Mary Hill" should read "Otto".
2. "Otto "(Shoal Lake) should read "Mary Hill".
3. Stefan M. Jonasson is currently (1984) archivist and chaplain in the Unitarian-Universalist Church of Winnipeg.

Appendix J

Icelandic Students and Graduates of Meadville Theological School, 1844-1944₁

//

The following biographical entries are listed in chronological order of graduation or departure from the school:

1856: ***TROWBRIDGE BRIGHAM FORBUSH.₂**
Graduate, 1856.
Born, Westboro, Mass., Jan. 15, 1832. Unitarian ministry. Northboro, Mass., associate pastor, Ord., Jan. 1, 1857-July 1, 1863; West Roxbury, July 1, 1863-May 1, 1868; Cleveland, O., May 17, 1868-June, 1876; Supt., Chicago Athenaeum, Chicago, ILL., May 1876-1880; Detroit, Mich., May 1, 1880-May, 1886; Milwaukee, Wis., May 1, 1886-Oct. 1, 1889; Western Supt., A.U.A., Oct. 1, 1889-Sept. 30, 1896; Memphis, Tenn., 1896-. Died, Memphis, Tenn., Jan. 6, 1898. See: Y.B., 1899, p.8. Heralds, vol. ii, p. 212. C.R., Jan. 13, 1898, p. 57.

1902: ***ROGNVALDUR PETURSSON.**
Graduate, 1902. D.D., 1928.
Born, Ripur, Skagafjartharsysla, Iceland, Aug. 14, 1877. Ph.D., Univ. of Iceland, 1929. Unitarian ministry. Winnipeg, Manitoba, Canada, First Icelandic Unitarian Church, July 1, 1903-(Ord., Aug. 2, 1903)-1909, 1915-1922; Field Missionary, Icelandic Unitarian Conference of Manitoba and the Northwest, Sept. 1, 1909-. Preached at Mary Hill, 1908-1911; Arnes, 1909-1922; Hnausa, 1909-1922; Shoal Lake, 1909-1910; Gimli, 1915-1922; Hecla, 1917-1922; 1937-1939; and Piney, 1921-1940, all in Manitoba, and at Kandahar, 1929-1936, and Kristnes, 1929-1936, in Saskatchewan, Canada. Founder and President, Icelandic National League; Editor, Iceland National Magazine. Died, Winnipeg, Man., Feb. 15, 1940. See: Y.B., 1940-1941, p. 157.

*Deceased as of date of publication in 1945.

1902: *JOHANN PJETUR SOLMUNDSSON.
Student, 1899-1902.
Born Heggestodum, Borgarfjord, Iceland, Sept. 28, 1872.
M.A., Univ. of Manitoba, 1923. Unitarian ministry. Winnipeg,
Man., Can., Sept. 28, 1902-1903; Gimli, Man., installed, Aug.
2, 1903-1910. Died, Gimli, Man., Mar. 25, 1935.
See: Y.B., 1935-1936, p. 133.

1908: *GUDMUNDUR ARNASON.
B.D., 1908.
Born, Borgarfjordur, Iceland, Apr. 4, 1880. Cruft Fellow, 1908-
1909. Winnipeg, Manitoba, Canada. First Icelandic Unitarian
Church, Ord., and installed, Sept. 19, 1909-Aug., 1915. In
Charge of churches in Lundar District, Manitoba, 1928-1943;
(Mary Hill, 1929-1943; Oak Point, 1929-1943; Shoal Lake,
1929-1943; Hayland, 1935-1943; Reykjavik, 1935-1943; Steep
Rock, 1935-1943; Hecla, 1941-1943; and Langruth, 1941-1943).
President, United Conference of Icelandic Churches in North
America; Regional Director, American Unitarian Association.
Died, Lundar, Manitoba, Feb. 24, 1943.
See: Y.B.,1943-1944, p. 92.

1910: *SIGURJON JONSSON.
Graduate, 1910.
Born, Nordurmulasysla, Iceland, Aug. 23, 1881. M.A., Univ. of
Chicago, 1913; Teacher, Reykjavik, Iceland; Grad. of
Theological School, Univ. of Reykjavik, 1917. Luth. ministry.
Ord., 1917; Bardin-Fljotum, Skagafjardsysla, 1917-1920;
Kirkjubae, Hroarstunga, S. Mulasysla, 1920-.

1910: ALBERT EDWARD KRISTJANSSON.
B.D., 1910.
Born, Husavik, Iceland, Apr. 23, 1878. Unitarian ministry.
Gimli, Manitoba, Canada, Ord. and installed, Sept. 25, 1910-
1913; Missionary work in Manitoba: at Mary Hill, 1913-1928;
at Shoal Lake, 1913-1928; at Hove, 1917-1926; at Oak Point,
1927-1928; Seattle, Wash.,(Icelandic Liberal Church), Oct.,
1928-1941; Seattle (First Church), 1931-1932; Blaine,
Washington, (Icelandic Free Church), 1928-1943.
Residence, Blaine, Wash.

1915: **OLAFUR KJARTANSSON.**
Student, 1914-1915.
Born, Skal, Sida District, Skaftafellssysla, Iceland, June 20, 1886. P.h.B., Univ. of Chicago, 1918. Teacher. Residence, Brooklyn, N.Y.

1916: **GUNNLOGUR BJORNSSON.**
Student, 1915-1916.
Born, Hunavatnssysla, Iceland, June 20, 1886. Residence, Chicago, Ill.

1929: **PHILIP MARKUS PETURSSON.**
Graduate, 1929. B.D., 1932.
Born, Roseau Co., Minn., Oct. 21, 1902. Ph.B., Univ. of Chicago, 1929. Univ. of Iceland, 1934-1935. Unitarian ministry. Winnipeg, Manitoba, Can., 1929-(installed, Winnipeg, Sept. 8, 1935)-.

1929: **FRIDRIK ADALSTEINN FRIDRIKSSON.**
Student, 1929.
Born, Reykjavik, Iceland, June 17, 1896. Graduate in Arts, State Coll. of Iceland, 1916; Grad. in Theology, Univ. of Iceland, 1921. Lutheran ministry. Ord., Reykjavik, Oct. 9, 1921. Unitarian ministry. Wynyard circuit of our congregations, Wynyard, Sask., Can., 1921-1930; Kandahar, Sask., 1927-1928; Kristnes, 1927-1928; Blaine, Wash., Apr. 1, 1930-1933. Returned to Iceland.

1936: **HELGI INGIBERG SIGURDUR BORGFORD.**
B.D., 1936.
Born, Winnipeg, Manitoba, Nov. 11, 1903. B.Sc., Univ. of Manitoba, 1927. Universalist ministry. Halifax, Nova Scotia (Church of the Redeemer), Ord., Jan. 12, 1937-1940. Unitarian ministry. Ottawa, Canada, 1940-.

1. These biographical entries were extracted from F.L. Weis: **General Catalogue of the Meadville Theological School** (Chicago: Meadville Theological School 1945) 150 pp. The following abbreviations appear in the entries to identify frequently-cited sources:

Heralds.   **Heralds of a Liberal Faith**. Edited by Samuel A. Eliot. 3 volumes. Boston 1910.

C.R.   **The Christian Register**. Weekly, 1821-1942; monthly since 1942. Boston.

Y.B.   **The Unitarian Year Book**. Published annually by the American Unitarian Association, Boston.

2. Although not Icelandic, T.B. Forush was involved prominently in the establishment of the Unitarian congregation in Winnipeg. He is included in this list because of his strong influence.

ELJ

Appendix K

Key toThe Icelandic Alphabet

The Icelandic alphabet consists of 36 letters, being comprised of the 26 letters of the English alphabet, seven others which are accented vowels, and three more which also appear in other alphabets. Incidentally, although they are included in the Icelandic alphabet, the letters 'c', 'q', and 'w' are rarely if ever used in Icelandic words.

The sequence of the letters follows:

A Á B C D Ð E É F G H I Í J K L M N O Ó
a á b c d ð e é f g h i í j k l m n o ó
P Q R S T U Ú V W X Y Ý Z Þ Æ Ö
p q r s t u ú v w x y ý z þ æ ö

Pronunciation Guide

Icelandic is a phonetic language with the names of the letters reflected precisely in their sounds.

	English equiv.
á pronounced as "ow" in "how"	a
ð pronounced as "th" in "rather". It never appears as an initial letter in a word or syllable.	d
é pronounced as "ye" in "yellow"	e
í pronounced as "ee" in "meet"	i
ó pronounced as long "o" in English e.g. "hope"	o
ú pronounced as "ou" in "you"	u
ý used as a vowel similar "i" above.	y
þ named "þorn" (thorn) sounds like "th" in "Thor"	th
æ pronounced as long "i" in English e.g. "side" (used as a vowel)	ae
ö a vowel pronounced as "u" in "utter"	o
ei a dipthong pronounced as "a" in "late"	ei
j consonant "j" pronounced as "y" in "yellow"	j

Epilogue

The Icelandic Unitarian Connection is, in truth, an unfinished story. Why, then, did I choose to publish it in its deficient state?

Within a few hours of the death of Emil Gudmundson, I began a gradual and systematic rational sifting of the many shared aspects of our diversified lives, in the prospect of setting some priorities for my future solo life. Suddenly, my mind came upon the reality of Emil's unfinished book. After a few moments of considering this major project, I knew it **must** be completed. Many were anticipating the book form of this absorbing story, especially those whose generous support underwrote Emil's research and lectures. Who could finish this research? Could I or someone else, and who was free to do so? My expertise in the sciences was not appropriate and my Icelandic language skills were insufficient unto the task, and I knew of no one appropriately skilled and free to work at the current time.

Thus, I resolved to take the responsibility for publishing Emil's book with no additional material other than from his fifth and sixth Minns lectures. My resolution to press ahead with publication was necessary but not sufficient to accomplish the task. More than "a little" help from my friends, relatives and publishers, however, **was** sufficient. Theirs be the glory, especially to Eric and Margaret Bjornson, Leslie Gudmundson, and Eric Jonasson in Manitoba, Helen Bullard in Tennessee and Conrad Wright and Carl Seaburg in Massachusetts.

It is my hope that the reader will record and discuss questions raised by reading text and appendices, and will actively seek answers to them. Take heed of the words on the University of Chicago seal: *Let knowledge grow from more to more, and so be human life enriched.* The great question, however, "What happened after 1900?" will have to be answered and elaborated by scholars yet to come forward. The papers of the Rev. Dr. V. Emil Gudmundson will eventually be located in the Archives of the Meadville/Lombard Theological School Library in Chicago. Emil told me as he was writing how sorry he was to have to leave so much interesting material out.

Succeeding historians of the Icelandic Unitarians in North America finding questions within these pages which will not let them rest, surely follow and write. I exhort them so to do.

- Barbara R. Gudmundson

About the Author

Valtýr Emil Gudmundson was born at "Borg" — the family farm — in the Mary Hill District near Lundar, Manitoba, on January 28, 1924. His father Björgvin Gudmundson, a farmer and fisherman, was a sensitive and jovial man. His mother, Rannveig, who had been a pioneer teacher for 12 years prior to her marriage, was respected for her teaching abilities and for her leadership in the church and community. Icelandic was Emil's only language until he entered elementary school.

Emil's allergies to hay and horses during his early years caused him to focus toward a life off the farm. His thoughts in liberal religion were fostered, discussed, and encouraged by his mother, his paternal grandmother, Mekkín Gudmundson, as well as by their minister, Guðmundur Árnason. During one summer vacation from the Lundar High School, he attended Unitarian Youth Camp at Hnausa, Manitoba. Emil was inspired, especially by the Rev. G. Richard Kuch — and was so challenged by Kuch that he decided then to become actively involved in the Unitarian movement. After a brief sojourn at the University of Manitoba, he taught grade school in a nearby district for one year, but found that teaching was not to his liking. As a consequence, he spent the war years working on the farm.

In 1945, he had the opportunity to obtain passage to Iceland aboard a newly built fishing boat bound there from North America. It was his intention to work his way across on the boat, but the unfortunate roughness of the North Atlantic in October precluding his doing so — and he spent most of the ten day crossing in distress on his bunk.

For the next two years, Emil was a student of the Theology Faculty of the University of Iceland. Between terms, he was able to visit his mother's relatives in Borgarfjörður in southwestern Iceland, and, during his last summer in Iceland, was able to visit his father's relatives in Borgarfjörður Eystri, far to the northeast.

In 1947, Emil returned to North America and enrolled in the University of Chicago, later attending Meadville Theological School there. In 1951, he and Barbara Rohrke, a Unitarian and a recent zoology graduate of the University of Tenessee, were married in Chicago's First Unitarian Church. During this time, he worked on completing his thesis in the field of Religion and Art, **Greek Rhetoric and Christian Preaching.** He received his B.D. degree from Meadville in 1952. In the ensuing years, Emil served as minister to churches in Maine, Connecticut (where his twin daughters were born), Texas — as well as Kristofer Janson's Norwegian Unitarian church in Hanska, Minnesota.

In January 1965, his life as an official representative of the denomination began when he was chosen to be its first District Executive by the newly-formed Prairie Star District of 65 churches and fellowships in the upper Midwest of the U.S.A. Later that year, in March 1965, he joined clergy from across the nation in the Freedom March in Selma, Alabama, to support equal rights for Black Americans. In 1970, in a major reorganization of the denomination, the Western Canada District and the Central Midwest District were added to Prairie Star, and Emil was appointed to be Interdistrict Representative of the Unitarian Universalist Association for the combined districts. His sensitivity to the religious needs of people and to the complex dynamics of each group with which he interacted, gave him a strong and positive reputation. In 1978, Meadville/Lombard Theological School honoured Emil by awarding him a Doctor of Divinity degree.

The scholarly side of his life occupied varying parts of his time, but was always present in his sermon preparations from the beginning of his ministry. However, during his years at the Hanska Church, he was able to devote more time to study and writing and, several years later, these scholarly activities gathered more momentum once his work as Interdistrict Representative began to show more pattern and predictability. After serving for 12 years within the Unitarian administration, he submitted his proposal for a study leave to research aspects of this book to U.U.A. President Paul Carnes early in 1978. During the five periods of study and sabbatical leave granted to him between fall 1978 and winter 1980, he researched primary historical sources at the University of Manitoba, Harvard Divinity School, Landbókasafn Íslands in Iceland, and the Icelandic Collection of Cornell University.

During the rare occasions when he had two or three days off at once, he concentrated his energies on the preparation of this book. The only significant deviation from this path occurred in March 1981 when he presented at the Winnipeg and Arborg Unitarian Churches the six Minns Lectures dealing with the topic of his research. His concentration focused on this work until the fall of 1982. His untimely death in December of 1982 at the farm on which he was born closed the circle of his life — and cut short a life committment to the propagation of the excitement of liberal religion.

BJRG

Index